THE IMPACT OF INFLUENCE VOLUME 8

Lessons Learned From Influencers

By

Chip Baker

Co-authored by Powerful Influencers

2024

THE
IMPACT

LESSONS LEARNED

OF

FROM INFLUENCERS

INFLUENCE

VOLUME 8

WRITTEN BY

CHIP BAKER

CO-AUTHORED BY POWERFUL INFLUENCERS

First Printing: 2024

ISBN: 979-8-3325188-7-4

Ordering Information:

Special discounts are available on quantity purchases by corporations, associations, educators, and others. For details, contact the publisher at the email listed below.

U.S. trade bookstores and wholesalers:
Please contact chipbakertsc@gmail.com.

DEDICATION

This book is dedicated to all the people who have made a positive impact in our life. We send a special dedication to our families and everyone who supports us. We hope that this book will help you influence and impact the people in your life! Go get it!

PREFACE

Dear reader,

We hope that this book will be a blessing to you. In the following chapters, you will find the lessons that these powerful authors have learned throughout their journey to success. Our hope is that you will learn from these lessons and use them to help you operate more efficiently and effectively in your life.

A Brief Description of this Book

The Impact of Influence Vol. 8, Lessons Learned from Influencers is overflowing with wisdom from visionary author, Chip Baker, and other powerful influencers who have discovered their paths to success. They are influencing many and impacting generations. The inspirational stories within the pages of this book will inspire you to make a positive difference for those around you.

TABLE OF CONTENTS

LIST OF AUTHORS IN CHAPTER ORDER

1. Chip Baker
2. Adrian P. Jackson
3. Dr. Brandi Brotherton
4. D'Andre J. Lacy
5. Dan Blanchard
6. David Settle
7. Derrick Pearson
8. Fendi Onobun
9. JD Hurd
10. Jose Escobar
11. Kenneth Morris
12. Ramon Chinyoung Sr.
13. Dr. Zandra Jo Galvan

YOUR ROI DETERMINES YOUR ROI
Chip Baker

"Everybody we meet has an influence on us and an impact - good or bad. And I think that's why we have to be careful with the way we handle people because what we're doing is making an impact."
~ *Ernie Harwell*

Influence and impact are powerful words because they demand strong actions. Influence comes in many forms and affects us through our daily interactions, shaping who we are. I have encountered numerous situations that have influenced and impacted me. I consider these situations as "radars of influence" – focused periods in specific environments. These radars of influence encompass the areas, communities, people, and situations we are blessed to be around. Because I chose to invest energy and effort into striving to be the best version of myself and helping others, I have been influenced and impacted in profound ways. I am truly grateful for these experiences, as they have taught me much about life.

In life, it is vital that we stretch ourselves and immerse in environments that will benefit us in the long run. This allows us to meet many great people and learn valuable lessons we can use to benefit others. Investing energy, effort, and placing ourselves in enriching environments yields an invaluable return, influencing and impacting generations.

"Your Radar of Influence (ROI) determines your Return on Investment (ROI). Your Return on Investment (ROI) determines your Radar of Influence (ROI)."
~ Chip Baker

In this chapter, I would like to reflect on my journey and how my personal radar of influence determined the return on my investments. I will also discuss how our radar of influence shapes our return on investment.

From High School to College

"Some of the most important decisions I have made might well have never been made or might have been very different if it hadn't been for the influence of the people in my life. We all need mentors."
~ Tony Clark

I was blessed to grow up in a great community filled with people who positively influenced my life. It was a small, close-knit community where everyone knew everyone. My mother involved me in many activities, such as community volunteering, school athletics, and church events. In high school, I had the privilege of playing four sports for four years, which provided priceless experiences.

I then went to college, played football, and earned my bachelor's degree. The college I chose, West Texas A&M University, was about a nine-hour drive from my hometown. Initially, I had reservations because it was so far away, but I had to overcome them for the incredible opportunity awaiting me.

At West Texas A&M University, I didn't know anyone at first, but it seemed like a great fit. The blessing of this experience was that my investments as a kid and high school student had prepared me for college. I only realized this as I was nearing the completion of my degree.

During my time at college I met many great people. They were from all over the world and became part of my radar of influence. I learned an abundance of knowledge from them, and this experience taught me about life and myself. I developed strong relationships and have friends I am still in contact with today. This radar of influence had a significant positive impact on me.

From College to a Career in Education

"As a person on planet Earth, you are capable of influencing another with your journey."
~ Rachel D. Greenwell

After college, I started working in education, an opportunity that arose from the lessons learned in my radar of influence and the investments of time, energy, and effort during my childhood and college years.

As I neared graduation, I applied for teaching and coaching positions in several school districts. One junior high school expressed significant interest. During reference checks, the principal discovered a mutual connection: my Little League Baseball Coach and Elementary School Principal, who was a pillar in my hometown and crucial in my radar of influence as a kid.

This administrator spoke highly of me, leading to my first teaching and coaching job. This opportunity stemmed from the person I was as a child, emphasizing that our daily actions are noticed and bring future opportunities.

This role allowed me to join an amazing school and district in a new area, surrounded by great thought leaders and trendsetters. I developed meaningful relationships with coworkers, families, and students. My radar of influence grew, bringing a significant return on my early investments.

I eventually had a 25-year career in education, was twice named Teacher of the Year on my campus, and received other accolades. I am still in education and love it. It has been a blessing to me, my loved ones, and the communities I serve. Reflecting on my journey, I realize the transferable skills I've learned prompted me to explore new interests.

From a Career in Education to Social Media Content Creation

As we navigate different radars of influence and invest in our growth, the transferable skills we acquire are invaluable. I love music, engaging in meaningful conversations, and highlighting people doing great things. These interests led me to create "Chip Baker - The Success Chronicles," a YouTube channel and podcast featuring interviews with people from all walks of life, sharing their stories for positive inspiration and motivation.

Starting this channel and podcast expanded my radar of influence, bringing many great experiences. I met and interviewed people worldwide and appeared on various podcasts. Though I had never created content before, my burning desire to make it happen and determination to learn drove me to succeed. This endeavor became another way to serve others and leave a legacy my family could be proud of.

Quality relationships I developed along the journey turned into strong support. I am truly grateful for their support. One influencer/author I met through content creation asked if I had considered writing a book. With his coaching, we co-authored my first two books. This journey, now on my 20th book, began with stretching myself to elevate to another radar of influence, yielding phenomenal returns.

The Importance of Positive Influences in Our Lives

"He who influences the thought of his times, influences all the times that follow. He has made his impress on eternity."
~ Hypatia

Positive influences are crucial for our personal growth, well-being, and success. They come from people, experiences, or environments that support and encourage us to become our best selves. Here are some reasons why positive influences are important:

1. **Inspiration and Motivation:** Positive influences inspire us to pursue our passions and motivate us to take action towards our goals.

2. **Role Models:** They provide role models who demonstrate positive values, behaviors, and attitudes, teaching us how to navigate life's challenges.

3. **Support System:** Positive influences offer a supportive network that helps us navigate difficult times, providing emotional support, guidance, and encouragement.

4. **Personal Growth:** They help us develop new skills, build confidence, and cultivate a growth mindset, leading to self-improvement.

5. **Positive Reinforcement:** Positive influences reinforce healthy behaviors and attitudes, helping us develop constructive habits and thought patterns.

6. **Better Decision-Making:** They help us make informed decisions that align with our values and goals.

7. **Resilience:** Positive influences help us develop resilience, enabling us to bounce back from setbacks and overcome obstacles.

8. **Improved Mental Health:** They can reduce stress, anxiety, and depression by promoting a positive outlook and supportive environment.

9. **Networking Opportunities:** Positive influences can introduce us to new people, experiences, and opportunities, expanding our network and horizons.
10. **Legacy:** Positive influences can leave a lasting legacy, inspiring future generations to follow in their footsteps.

Surrounding ourselves with positive influences profoundly impacts our lives, helping us become the best version of ourselves and achieve our full potential. Your ROI determines your ROI!

God bless you on your journey to expand your radars of influence. You will see a tremendous return on your investment.

Go get it!

ABOUT THE AUTHOR:

See Lead Author's Bio in About the Author section.

REFLECTIONS FROM THE RIVER VALLEY: A JOURNEY OF LEADERSHIP, PERSEVERANCE, AND PURPOSE

Adrian Jackson

Among my most cherished pastimes is the peaceful joy of horseback riding through the Canadian River Valley in the Texas Panhandle, a lush and tranquil place where I immerse myself in the sights, sounds, and smells of nature. The smooth, fluid motion of Champ, my Tennessee Walking Horse, allows me to reflect on the events that have shaped my days, months, and years. In these moments of introspection, I often smile when I think about where I started and where I am now. Simply enjoying this moment of solitude with nature embodies all that I have strived for. I ponder countless experiences that have enriched my life, the bonds of friendship and love that have been tenderly nurtured, and the triumphs that have illuminated my path. Yet, amidst these reflections, there are moments where I shed a solitary tear for the loved ones I've lost, the mentors who've passed, and the struggles that have plagued our nation. Many lessons learned and the "stupid tax" paid due to less-than-ideal decisions have been integral parts of my success.

Born and raised in the housing projects of north Lake Charles, Louisiana, my parents instilled strong values in my eight siblings and me. These values—emphasizing education, hard work, dedication, follow-through, consistency, and discipline—served as the foundation of our success. My parents' commitment to education propelled eight of us to achieve college degrees, a remarkable feat that included two sisters who earned Juris Doctor degrees. For us, basketball wasn't just a game; it was a gateway to higher education. Personally, I count myself blessed to have received a basketball scholarship to Clarendon College, where I earned my associate degree and married the love of my life, Telita. Continuing my academic and athletic journey, Telita and I transferred to Oklahoma Panhandle State University in Goodwell, OK, where I pursued and earned my bachelor's degree in business administration. I am filled with admiration for my parents' resilience in raising nine children on a modest income. Despite facing financial constraints, they ensured our lives were filled with cherished family traditions. Their ability to achieve so much with so little continues to serve as a profound source of inspiration in my life.

There were countless lessons ingrained in me during my formative years at 1341 Kirk Ave, but one lesson was imparted not through verbal instruction, but through the silent eloquence of actions. It was the profound testament of my father's unwavering dedication and tireless work ethic that left an indelible impression on me. Witnessing my father's relentless efforts to provide for his family, through his actions, my father taught me the invaluable lesson of perseverance in the face of adversity and the importance of selflessness in caring for those we hold dear. His silent sacrifices spoke volumes, instilling in me a profound sense of gratitude, resilience, and empathy. As I reflect on those defining moments of my upbringing, his role modeling of protecting, providing for, and loving one's family was deeply ingrained in me, guiding my actions and decisions as a husband from a young age.

Today, as I reflect on those challenging yet formative years, I am grateful for the lessons learned and the values instilled within me. They have shaped me into the person I am today—a devoted husband, a loving father, and a diligent worker, committed to providing a better future for my family, just as my father did before me. My mother and father had vastly different approaches, yet they were equally intentional in the lessons they wanted us to learn. While my mother focused on preparing me for adulthood—teaching me things like formal dining etiquette, appropriate attire for various occasions, and how to interact respectfully with people from different cultures—she also emphasized skills like public speaking, financial management, and presenting oneself in a professional manner. The way I carry myself today reflects the traits and characteristics instilled in me by both my mother and father. I am indebted to their intentionality in guiding not only me but also my eight siblings to become the individuals we are today.

Telita and I transitioned to Cal Farley's Boys Ranch, a residential community dedicated to providing care and support for at-risk children, as house parents in an adolescent boys' home when I was just 22 years old—only a few years older than the oldest student in our care and one of the youngest employees on campus. I had no idea what experiences lay ahead for us. One of my early supervisors, Steve Nelson, greatly influenced my supervisory style. He approached his role with a strong sense of purpose, taking ownership of personally training his staff and role-modeling that training. Steve was always the first to intervene with a student overwhelmed with emotions, adhering meticulously to the structured training curriculum mandated by the organization. He also expected the same level of commitment and adherence from us, setting a high standard for effective and compassionate supervision. Steve's relentless expectation that his staff be the best at working with the most challenging youth on campus propelled my career and set the tone for all the events that followed.

Another influential mentor, Mark Strother, provided crucial leadership guidance. Introducing me to Life Space Crisis Intervention (LSCI) marked a significant turning point in my career. His emphasis on embracing diverse perspectives to tackle complex organizational challenges was invaluable. Under his guidance, I learned to approach issues with a broader viewpoint, enhancing my ability to manage and support the youth in our care and develop staff into leaders within the organization. Mark's influence molded my leadership style, emphasizing empathy, strategic thinking, and comprehensive problem-solving. Michelle Maikoetter was another leader who had a profound impact on my leadership style. Under her guidance, my professional development has advanced considerably.

Michelle's impact on my leadership growth was profound. She refined my skills by sharing valuable insights and perspectives, guiding me toward a deeper understanding of effective leadership. One crucial lesson she imparted was the importance of positional power, a concept I had previously taken for granted. Michelle helped me grasp how to respectfully acknowledge positional power and the responsibilities it entails within an organization. Moreover, she modeled a remarkable level of compassion in her high-ranking position, setting a standard that I aspire to emulate. Michelle demonstrated genuine care and concern for each employee and their loved ones, fostering an environment of empathy and respect that I strive to uphold in my own leadership role.

I am profoundly grateful for the leadership, mentorship, and friendship of Steve, Mark, and Michelle. Their unwavering support and guidance have been instrumental in shaping my career, enabling me to positively influence the lives of the students in our care and become a more effective and compassionate leader to my staff. Their impact on my professional and personal development is immeasurable, and I am deeply thankful for their enduring presence in my journey. Without their leadership and investment in my growth, I would not be able to positively impact others and offer them the same support and guidance that I received.

In my journey of personal and professional growth, I have identified three guiding principles that have consistently proven invaluable, regardless of the circumstances. These insights, drawn from the lessons taught by my mother, father, and mentors, can be distilled into three fundamental points: (1) Be Teachable, (2) Be Reachable, and (3) Be Respectable. Whether I am working with the students at Boys Ranch or guiding my staff through their growth, these fundamental qualities come to light. When you add all the lessons together, plus my experience as a collegiate athlete, these qualities merge to form a cohesive framework for success.

1. Be Teachable

Being teachable embodies a mindset of continuous learning and growth, epitomizing the ethos of "Always be a student," as my mentor, Steve, often emphasized. This principle fosters humility and the recognition that improvement is perpetual. In my work with students at Boys Ranch, this mindset allows me to adapt to their unique needs and refine my approach constantly. As a leader, it involves creating an environment where staff can thrive, fostering their personal and professional growth.

Accepting feedback is a cornerstone of being teachable. It entails actively listening to others' perspectives, comprehending their insights, and integrating their suggestions into one's practice. This mindset perceives feedback as a vehicle for growth rather than a personal critique. By adopting this approach, feedback transforms into actionable steps that propel significant improvements and lead to success.

By embodying the principles of continuous learning and growth, you demonstrate humility and a willingness to embrace new knowledge and experiences. This enriches your own development and inspires others to adopt a similar approach. When you actively encourage and exemplify the value of being teachable, you create an environment where others feel supported and empowered to do the same. Your openness to feedback and willingness to adapt to new perspectives instill confidence in your peers and mentors alike, signaling maturity and commitment to improvement. Your teachable demeanor communicates that you are receptive to guidance and expertise, fostering trust and encouraging investment in your growth. Nurturing a culture of teachability within your community, school, or organization enhances individual learning and growth, fostering a collaborative and supportive environment where everyone's potential can flourish. Ultimately, this collective commitment to continuous improvement promotes excellence, innovation, and positive impact within the milieu.

2. Be Reachable

Michelle truly embodies the trait of being reachable, which goes beyond mere physical accessibility. It's about being open and approachable in every interaction, demonstrating emotional availability and a willingness to engage meaningfully with others. Being reachable involves fostering open lines of communication and being responsive to the needs and inquiries of those around you.

In my experience as a youth care worker, I've learned that being reachable is essential for establishing trust with our students. By embodying professionalism and approachability, I've created an atmosphere where students feel safe, valued, and understood. When you're reachable, it creates an environment where ideas can be shared, problems can be addressed, and relationships can be nurtured.

In a leadership role, being reachable means being approachable, responsive, empathetic, and transparent. It's about creating an environment where team members feel comfortable reaching out, getting timely responses, feeling understood, and being informed. These traits promote teamwork, a positive work environment, and overall team success.

3. Be Respectable

At the heart of my upbringing, instilled by my parents, is the vital principle of being respectable. It's not merely about earning respect through words, but rather through genuine actions grounded in integrity, honesty, and dignity. This understanding has led me to realize that true respect for others starts with respecting oneself—a profound truth that shapes all interpersonal dynamics. Self-respect is the cornerstone of recognizing one's inherent worth and the value of treating others with dignity and compassion. This awareness forms the basis for nurturing healthy relationships and personal well-being.

At Boys Ranch, this principle is central to our approach in creating a positive environment for our students. By exemplifying kindness, fairness, and accountability, we establish a standard of behavior that fosters trust and admiration within our community. In my leadership role, I emphasize the importance of integrity and doing what's right, even in challenging circumstances. This commitment to respect and honesty not only earns the trust of my peers but also lays the foundation for enduring relationships based on mutual respect and admiration.

Furthermore, honoring the contributions of trailblazers like Mark, Steve, and Michelle is essential. Mark had a unique way of demonstrating the respectful honoring of those who carved the unpaved road. His visionary leadership and willingness to challenge norms inspire us to continue their legacy of innovation and growth. By acknowledging their achievements and learning from their experiences, we ensure the continuity and advancement of our community, guided by the wisdom of those who came before us.

In conclusion, my journey has been profoundly shaped by the unwavering support of my parents and the invaluable guidance of influential mentors. Regardless of one's chosen career path, the wisdom gleaned from others is indispensable. Surrounding oneself with like-minded individuals who share similar values and aspirations can be remarkably empowering. Together, uplifting and inspiring each other, propelling to new heights of growth and achievement. Prioritizing spiritual, personal, and professional development, we embrace a holistic approach to self-improvement, leading to a more fulfilling and balanced life. These principles of being teachable, reachable, and respectable have served as guiding lights on my life journey, and I am deeply grateful for the relationships forged along the way, as well as the unwavering support of my wife, Telita. As I reflect on my experiences, my heartfelt desire is to pay forward the wisdom I've gained. Through this, I aspire to influence the next generation of impactful leaders, fostering a legacy characterized by growth, compassion, and excellence that transcends my own journey.

ABOUT THE AUTHOR:

Social Media:

Facebook facebook.com/AdrianJackson

Email adrianjackson0187@yahoo.com

Adrian Jackson, originally from Lake Charles, Louisiana, and a graduate of Washington-Marion High School, excelled as a student-athlete in collegiate-level basketball. He earned his associate degree from Clarendon College and a bachelor's in business administration from Oklahoma Panhandle State University. Since 1997, Adrian and his wife Telita have been integral members of Cal Farley's Boys Ranch, initially serving as house parents in an adolescent boys' home.

Over the years, Adrian has held various pivotal roles within the organization, showcasing his dedication and adaptability. He has served as Director of Intervention Services and School Support, as well as Assistant Administrator of Intervention and Special Programs. Currently, as Vice President of Homelife, Adrian oversees departments such as Adventure, Intervention Team Services, Recreation, and others, aiming to create a nurturing environment for the children.

Adrian's commitment to professional growth is underscored by his certifications in childcare administration and various intervention programs. His journey reflects a deep-seated passion for youth service and continuous efforts to refine his skills in child welfare, positively impacting the lives of the children under his care.

In addition to his professional endeavors, Adrian is a seasoned professional bird dog trainer, recognized for winning numerous championships and national awards. He is respected in the pointing dog field trial community as a judge. Adrian and Telita are proud parents of three children and doting grandparents to two cherished grandchildren.

POWER IN YOUR CALLING
Dr. Brandi Brotherton

My name is Dr. Brandi Godino-Brotherton. I hail from Booker, TX, a small town with just over 1,000 people. Believe it or not, I graduated high school with just 32 kids—yes, 32! I am the proud descendant of my grandparents, Dovie and Calvin Cochran, and Alfredo and Antonia Godino.

My journey began with my mom becoming pregnant with me at just 18 years old, and my parents, being kids themselves, were not prepared. My grandparents had never dreamed of going to college. In fact, my paternal grandfather, Grandpa Godino, only attended school until the 6th grade, and my grandmother taught herself to read as an adult. My father entered kindergarten not knowing any English and was unfairly labeled as dumb and illiterate. Witnessing the discrimination against my father, my grandmother made a vow that no one in her family would speak Spanish at home to shield us from the same ridicule she and my father endured. Thus, we never did. My parents were high school graduates, and back then, that was considered good enough for both their families and society.

Skipping forward, I excelled academically and athletically in high school. I was an exceptional student and an even better basketball player, earning all-state honors my junior year. However, my senior year, everything changed when I tore my ACL, MCL, meniscus, and cracked my kneecap—all from a non-contact injury during a basketball game. At that moment, my life's focus shifted dramatically. Although Baylor University still expressed interest in me despite my injuries, I chose to decline their offer and leave basketball behind. It was a difficult decision, but sometimes in life, you have to say no, change direction, and choose yourself.

After high school, I attended Oklahoma State University and later pursued law school in Houston, Texas. However, my aspirations of becoming a high-powered lawyer like Johnny Cochran were derailed when I realized that making money in law meant specializing in oil and gas, torts, or contract law—none of which interested me. Despite the pressure from my family and hometown to succeed, I made the hard decision to quit law school and follow a different path. It was the second time in my life that I chose myself over external expectations, and it set the stage for my future endeavors.

I eventually found my calling at Elsik High School in Houston, the 8th largest school in Texas. I landed my dream job coaching girls' basketball, which required me to also teach. This experience marked the beginning of my real mission. Although I was initially overwhelmed by the size of the school and the number of students, I quickly adapted and found my stride. My passion for education grew, and I realized that teaching and leading young minds were my true calling.

Reflecting on my journey, I was destined to be a difference-maker and an educator. Despite the doubts and challenges along the way, I earned my Masters in Education and eventually became part of the .4% of Hispanic women in the US with a Doctoral Degree. This achievement is not just a personal triumph but a testament to breaking the cycle of educational barriers within my family and community.

Being the first in my family to attend college, earn a master's, and achieve a doctorate has set a new standard for future generations. It's about leaving a legacy and paving the way for others who come after me. I often remind my students to believe in themselves, even when others may not, and to align their choices and work ethic with the life they aspire to create.

Throughout my journey, I've been supported by my family, friends, and mentor, Hilda Rodriguez, who believed in me before I believed in myself. Their unwavering belief and investment in my potential shaped me into the leader and educator I am today. Now, as the proud principal of a National Blue Ribbon School, I strive to inspire and support my teachers and students every day.

In conclusion, my story is not just about personal achievement but about the impact we can have on others when we follow our passions and stay true to ourselves. I am grateful for the opportunities I've had to make a difference and to leave a lasting legacy as a Hispanic woman who defied the odds.

ABOUT THE AUTHOR:

Social Media:
LinkedIn linkedin.com/in/brandi-brotherton/
Facebook facebook.com/profile.php?id=61553870652155
Email brotherton.brandi@gmail.com

Dr. Brotherton brings over 20 years of experience in public education to her role. She earned her Bachelor of Arts in Political Science from Oklahoma State University, her Masters in Educational Administration from Abilene Christian University, and her Doctorate in Educational Leadership and Innovation from St. Thomas University. Based in Houston, Texas, Dr. Brotherton has excelled in various roles including high school teacher, coach, advanced academic coordinator, assistant principal, associate principal of instruction, and currently serves as principal at a National Blue Ribbon High School.

Known as the "Culture Queen," Dr. Brotherton is celebrated for her transformative leadership style that uniquely engages and connects the school community. She firmly believes that strong relationships form the bedrock of successful school outcomes, emphasizing the critical role leaders play in fostering and sustaining a positive school culture. Dr. Brotherton is dedicated to developing and empowering leaders with the essential skills to create environments that nurture both teacher and student success.

Under her leadership, Dr. Brotherton has achieved remarkable milestones including leading the #1 Rated Gold Ribbon High School in Texas, significantly improving "Masters" scores on state assessments by 18% at her campus, and managing one of the highest-performing Title I schools in the state. Yet, her greatest professional achievement lies in establishing and maintaining a campus culture that fosters thriving outcomes for teachers and students alike.

ONE MIC
D'Andre J. Lacy

"Yo, all I need is one mic, one beat, one stage…
…One God to show me how to do things his son did."
—Nasir Jones

All we need is one!
One thought!
One belief!
One moment!
One decision!
One person!
One yes!

We are all one thought, one belief, one moment, one decision, one person, and one yes away from changing our lives forever! The psalmist Jonathan Nelson sang, "I am just one praise from my breakthrough, I'm just one praise away from my blessing!" Little did I know, over 15 years ago, that I would realize this in my own life. I made a decision to ignore my doubts and fears, step out in faith, and changed the trajectory of my life forever.

My name is D'Andre J. Lacy. I am a husband, a father, a minister, an international public speaker, and the Amazon best-selling author of Out of the Ashes: Finding the Purpose in Your Pain.

I have had the amazing opportunity to travel the world and share my messages of hope and inspiration. But before I became who I am today, I was a boy with low self-esteem, high anxiety, PTSD, living every day in fear.

Before the actual life-changing moment, a seed was planted that would facilitate that transformation. In my book, I write about a traumatic experience I endured in 6th grade. Due to this, my extended family took a special interest in supporting me, encouraging me, and building my confidence. One thing my aunt, uncle, his wife, and my grandparents did was take me with them during the summer so I had time away from home to see something different, clear my mind, and spend time with my cousins.

In the summer of 2008, I attended an event with my cousin and uncle called Freestyle Friday. My uncle, now a pastor, who was a youth pastor at the time, created the event to give young teens an outlet to use their gifts, worship, learn about God, and have a safe place to congregate and have fun. Part of the night was a talent show of sorts. One of the young men, Michael Wayne, a friend and church member, was a Christian rap artist and encouraged my cousin to do the same. One day, my cousin was working on a song titled "Freestyle Friday" and asked me to rap on it with him. I was hesitant at first, but with his encouragement, I began writing, and we recorded it. This was my verse:

> Servin' God's my only habit and it's plain to see
> If you not down with Jesus Christ, you need to get like me
> My cousin put me on this track cause I'm lyrically gifted
> And since I've been down with Christ, I've been spiritually lifted
> Livin' life with Christ puts you on another level
> If you not down with Christ, you gettin' played by the devil
> And if you runnin' with the devil, then you rollin' with a coward
> But I roll with Jesus Christ, He gives me eternal power

This was not the life-changing moment this chapter is about, but it was one of the sparks that led to the fire of my life-altering decision. I had always been creative, but I mostly kept it to myself and it was never consistently affirmed, so I did not see it as a gift or talent. This was the first time I had an opportunity to actually share something I was talented at with others. Unfortunately, I went back home and did not get to perform the song with them, but it did evoke a sense of accomplishment and confidence in me.

Eventually, fate would have it that I would permanently move to Houston with my uncle, aunt, and their children (my cousins). The move afforded me the opportunity to be in a new environment, which was the spark that started a shift for me psychologically. I am a firm believer in Maslow's Hierarchy of Needs. Visually, it is demonstrated as a pyramid that has physiological needs (breathing, food, water, shelter, clothing, sleep) at the bottom. Above that is safety and security (health, employment, property, family and social stability). The third tier is love and belonging (friendship, family, intimacy, sense of connection). The fourth level is self-esteem (confidence, achievements, respect of others, the need to be a unique individual). Finally, the peak of the pyramid is self-actualization (morality, creativity, spontaneity, acceptance, experience, purpose, meaning, and inner potential). The good news for me was that there wasn't a single level where I lacked all traits, but the unfortunate news was that the areas I did have gaps were so severe they overpowered the areas where I was sufficient.

This new environment provided the sense of safety I longed for, which empowered me to realize something: I was severely depressed, anxious, lacked confidence in myself, and was extremely limited in social settings. When you are in survival mode, processing emotions is a luxury. Your mind, body, and spirit are engulfed by the anxiety, terror, and stress of the source of your anguish, leaving no freedom to deal with the higher levels of Maslow's pyramid. I was always aware of the cloud of negativity that reigned over my mind, but this was the first time I had the space to realize it was a problem and it was impeding my progress in life. Fortunately, by living with my cousins, I was thrust into many more social situations with peers outside of school hours than I would have been back home. This positive peer pressure was great for my development and culminated in the moment that changed my life forever!

Let's fast-forward to 2009. At this point, I had been living in Houston for several months and had switched schools three times in a year's span. With my crippling anxiety and challenges with my mental health, being the new guy at school did not help things. I needed something to build my confidence and help me establish my identity. I wasn't looking for this moment, and it found me anyway.

Remember what I said earlier: You are one yes away from changing your life.

One thought.

One moment.

One decision.

I was at a youth event with my cousin and the newly formed Christian Rap Group G's for Jesus. My cousin, Michael, was a part of the group along with Michael Wayne, Jerrmie, and Big Swole (I can't remember his actual name, but that's what we called him). They were there to perform, and I was there to support them from the audience—or so I thought. Throughout the night, they were constantly telling me I should go on stage with them. I kept saying no. "Go on stage and do what?" I thought to myself. As each prior performer finished their act, I was running out of time to decide what I was going to do. I don't know why. I don't know how. It had to be God and the Holy Spirit. Somehow, I allowed them to convince me to go on stage with them.

I was nervous and instantly regretted my decision, but eventually, I relaxed. Unfortunately, we ran into technical difficulties. As we all stood before the crowd, something went wrong with the music and some of the mics. What I did next shocked the group and myself: I began to speak to fill the dead space while they corrected the issues. The issues with the music were resolved, and I went on to perform with the group. Soon after, I became an official member. I don't think those brothers realized how much I needed that at that time in my life and what that moment did for me and my confidence. We performed at several events around Houston, and I began to be more and more confident. Then, just as things seemed to be going well, there was a split in the group. I don't remember all the details, and honestly, I don't care to even attempt to remember. The gist of what happened is my cousin and I formed a separate group from the other three guys.

This is when I grew to another level. Due to my age and lack of a driver's license, I never actually got to be featured on any songs because I could never make it to a recording session. Plus, I was just added to the group, and honestly, I was just happy to be there. I was the person who warmed up the crowd before we performed and a hype man. With it just being my cousin and myself, I started recording raps and doing half of the verses on a song. I was required to contribute more.

Was I ready for this?

Would I let my cousin down?

Would I embarrass myself?

I know it was the Holy Spirit because when I performed, I became an entirely different person. On stage, I was bold, confident, loud, and charismatic. I would run into the crowd, jump up and down, and yell at the top of my lungs. It was like when Clark Kent went into the phone booth and became Superman. We continued to perform around Houston, recorded two mixtapes, performed at several events, and even rubbed shoulders with Still Trill Christians, AJ McQueen, J-flow, and other Christian Hip Hop artists at that time. Then, two seemingly tragic situations happened back-to-back: my cousin's recording equipment was stolen, and my cousin moved to Las Vegas for a job.

I was devastated. I felt like Peter Parker in the movie Spiderman Homecoming. There is a scene in which Tony Stark (Ironman), played by Robert Downey Jr., is taking back the suit he made for Spiderman (Tom Holland). Spiderman says, "But I'm nothing without the suit!" Ironman replies, "If you're nothing without the suit, then you shouldn't have it!" This scene is exactly how I felt when I realized my cousin and I were done making music. For once in my life, I finally felt like somebody. For once, I had found something I was good at, and it even inspired others. I was beginning to have confidence in myself and garnering more respect from my peers.

A particular memory of how my rapping changed people's perception of me happened after my cousin and I performed at a church that some of my high school classmates attended. I do not remember this girl's name, but I knew her from school. She came up to me and said, "I used to think you were lame, but now I see you're kind of cool." At the time, I wasn't sure how to feel about that backhanded compliment, but this entire situation taught me a few things that I would later understand:

My lack of confidence made me appear lame.

People were uncomfortable around me because I wasn't confident in myself.

People had met the PTSD version of me but hadn't met the real me.

I confused my gift with a manifestation of my gift.

The last lesson was the greatest one I learned from this situation, and I still carry it with me to this day. Our last performance was in 2010. I graduated in 2011 and went off to college. I accepted my call to preach in 2014 and began to understand the purpose of that season of my life.

Although I was always poetic, poetry was not my gift. I was always a writer, but that was not my gift either. At one point, I wanted to be a lawyer, but that was not God's plan for my life. Rapping was also a gift, but it was not THE gift. My gift was communication. My gift was wisdom. My gift was exhortation. Rapping was just how it was manifested at that time. Music was just the conduit for the messages God was speaking through me in that period. God was using all the skills required to rap to prepare me for my ministry of preaching, becoming an author, and eventually an international motivational speaker who recently spoke at a conference in Montreal, Quebec, Canada.

That season of rapping with my cousin was not an accident. That season of performing was not in vain. God used all of that to prepare me for a future I could not even see.

I dedicate this chapter to Michael Wayne. He knew he inspired me to rap and knew I became a preacher later, but I never got to sit down and truly share with him how much what he did for me meant. Had he not pushed my cousin to rap and asked me to do the same, I may have never discovered my purpose in life. Unfortunately, Michael, aka MC Mike Wayne, passed away in January 2024. He leaves behind a wife, son, and many family and friends who mourn his death.

I dedicate this chapter to him. We weren't close after we stopped making music. We only spoke when we happened to run into each other at events or online on social media, but he still had a tremendous impact on my life.

Don't confuse your gift with how the gift can be used. Your one gift can be expressed in many ways. Your pain has a purpose. Your pain is a compass to your destiny.

Don't create a life you have to escape. Define your core values. Discover your gift (the thing you do better than most with the least amount of effort). Find a problem you want to solve or a product or service you wish to offer the world. Finally, solve the problem while using your gift without violating your values.

That, my friend, is your purpose in life. You are here to do more than pay bills and die. You have a purpose, and God wants to use it to get the glory from your story.

Stop waiting for the perfect time. The time is now!

ABOUT THE AUTHOR:

Social Media:
LinkedIn linkedin.com/in/d-lacy/
Facebook facebook.com/DJLinspires
Email dandrejlacy@djlinspires.com

D'Andre J. Lacy is an international motivational speaker and the Amazon best-selling author of Out of the Ashes: Finding the Purpose in Your Pain, which debuted at #5 in the PTSD category. D'Andre has over a decade of experience engaging, educating, empowering, and inspiring audiences across diverse cultural, social, and ethnic backgrounds. This internationally known speaker has captivated crowds at universities, conferences, prisons, and churches.

FINDING MY VOICE: DEFYING EXPECTATIONS
Dan Blanchard

"Stop hitting him," pleaded my mom.

"He's not listening! And he will mind me," yelled my father.

I'm about two years old at this time, and my parents think I'm mentally retarded. They also thought my older brother Chris was stubborn and wouldn't listen or do what he was told. Chris and I didn't talk much. In fact, I wasn't really talking at all. I made animal noises and pointed at things. Our father ignored my mom and struck Chris again because he wasn't listening. My older sister Theresa was always caught in the middle, trying to help her two brothers. She was far more mature than Chris and me. She worried about us both, so she did what she could to help us get by in life.

Chris didn't listen to our father's commands because he couldn't hear them very well. Later in life, Theresa told me that Chris had somehow learned to read lips to some degree during that time of our lives. He followed her lead at other times to avoid some of the beatings.

I didn't get smacked around as much as Chris. Maybe it's because everyone thought I was mentally retarded. Back then, I just made a lot of animal noises. My parents didn't realize their two sons were hearing impaired.

Eventually, someone figured out Chris was partially deaf. Logical reasoning led my parents to wonder if I was deaf too. They tested me and found I was totally deaf. No wonder I had missed all the benchmarks of toddler development, including speaking.

The doctors told my parents they had good news and bad news. The good news was that an operation could fix both of their boys' hearing. However, their speech would be a different matter, especially for the younger one, me. Somehow, Chris learned how to talk pretty well for a kid who couldn't hear very well. So, he might get by with extensive speech lessons. But I, the one who maybe wasn't mentally retarded after all, still only made animal noises. And would, unfortunately, never learn to talk. The formative years of hearing sounds that naturally develop speech were robbed from me because, unlike my older brother, I couldn't hear anything. All the experts said it was too late for me to learn to speak. They told my parents I'd do nothing but make animal noises for the rest of my life.

My mom wouldn't accept it. As soon as I had recovered from my ear operation, she found an elderly nun who believed I could learn to talk. I religiously went to speech lessons where she wouldn't accept defeat.

I don't remember how long it took, but my mom, along with her steadfast belief in me, their religion, and the never-relenting efforts of that little old nun, created a miracle. I learned to speak.

Over the years, many people have asked me where I got my Boston accent from. My friends have even joked that the little old nun must have been an Italian nun from Boston. You see, I am a born and raised Connecticut native, but I often talk with my hands and have a mysterious Boston accent where I don't pronounce my R's. I have never lived in Boston. I've lived in Connecticut all my life. Who knows where the accent comes from... Maybe the little old nun was an Italian from Boston. Whoever she was, she and my mom and grandma were extraordinary people who wouldn't let this little boy fall by the wayside. I was going to talk and, someday, talk a lot. They made sure I had a fighting chance. They also had a growth mindset before a growth mindset was even a thing. They didn't think I was stuck with what I was born with. They knew I could do better than just making animal noises all my life. They were right.

Today, I am an inner-city schoolteacher, sports coach, author, and speaker. I'm always talking, every day, all day long. And sometimes my wife tells me I talk too much. And she might be right! The evidence is in her favor. I am always talking and often have a sore throat and hoarse voice. I might be guilty as charged. But I don't care because I used to be the little boy who everyone thought was mentally retarded and would only make animal noises. The lesson is that none of us are stuck. Every one of us can use a growth mindset to keep improving no matter where we come from or what we're up against.

Now, the road has sometimes been rocky. Over the years, I've also had many people tell me I talk funny. A lot of these people who told me that I talk weird had good intentions too. For example, a woman I got to know through being an author and speaker told me that I have to learn to stop talking funny, or no one will ever take me seriously in the professional speaking and author world. She told me I had to study the Midwestern newscasters on television. "They don't have an accent and speak clearly and professionally," she told me. She reminded me I'd only be short-changing myself until I learned to speak like them.

I watched a couple of their news reports and couldn't see myself ever talking like them. I know I talk funny—a lot of people have told me over the years that I talk funny. I also know I have an accent. Over the years, I've seen many heads turn to see who was speaking with that accent. But guess what? That's who I am. I'm the guy who has an accent and talks funny. But I don't care. That's who I am.

Hey, what can I say? I'm the guy who grew up in the 80s watching all the Blockbuster movies with Arnold Schwarzenegger and Sylvester Stallone talking funny too. And look how well they did while talking funny. All these years later, most of us still know Arnold's famous line, "I'll be back." And we also remember Rocky calling out, "Adrian! Adrian! Adrian!" after he fought Apollo Creed.

And no one discredited either of those massive Hollywood stars because they talked funny.

If they can talk funny and still do a great job reaching their potential, I can too, and so can you. My advice here is to just be yourself. Be authentic. Don't be a cheap copy of someone else. Just be yourself. No one else can be a better version of you than you.

So there you have it in a nutshell. No matter where you come from or what you're up against, you are not stuck with a fixed mindset. Use your growth mindset and improve your life. In addition, do it as the best version of yourself, your authentic self, even if that version sometimes looks a little funny or talks a little funny. None of that matters when you decide to reach out and grab your full potential.

Now, get out there and do the work to make it happen!

Dan Blanchard is a bestselling and award-winning author, speaker, educator, TV host, and philanthropist. Learn more about Dan: www.GranddaddysSecrets.com

ABOUT THE AUTHOR:

Social Media:

LinkedIn: linkedin.com/in/daniel-blanchard-i-help-young-people-become-good-people-82a69723/

FB: facebook.com/daniel.blanchard.186/

Email Dan007blanchard@gmail.com

Dan Blanchard- Bestselling, Award Winning Author, Speaker, Educator, Coach, TV Host, philanthropist, TEDx Speaker, two-time Junior Olympian Wrestler, and two-time Junior Olympian Coach who has been featured on several of the World's Top Ten podcasts. Dan has completed 14 years of college earned seven degrees and is a veteran of the Army and Air Force.

BEYOND THE BREAKUP: THE IMPACT OF DALELYNN SETTLE

David Settle

When I reflect on the idea of influence and the individuals who have profoundly impacted my life, numerous names come to mind. It's clear that no one reaches their destination alone. I've been fortunate to be surrounded by many impactful people who have shaped who I am today.

Of course, there are the expected influences like my grandmother or my dad, who have been foundational in my upbringing. My father and mother-in-law have been spiritual pillars, serving as my pastors and mentors. Additionally, I've had great coaches, teachers, and friends. However, for this chapter, I am narrowing it down to one remarkable person who embodies resilience and has taught me invaluable lessons.

In Houston, Texas, lives a remarkable woman named Dalelynn Settle. She happens to be the mother of my children and my ex-wife. Yes, you read that correctly—my ex-wife is arguably one of the most influential people I know. I've had a front-row seat to her incredible journey of defeating depression, overcoming obesity, and kicking anxiety in the butt!

Dalelynn achieved all of this while raising five children. She had every reason to give up, but she didn't. She faced each obstacle with perseverance and grace, never letting adversity hold her back.

One of the most challenging moments was losing her sister to an aortic dissection, yet she fought for her life and lost over half her body weight, even being featured in People Magazine for her incredible accomplishments.

Beyond her personal triumphs, Dalelynn has started businesses, traveled the world on mission trips, and faithfully served as a worship leader. She has taught me the meaning of faith and what true worship is all about. Even during our divorce, typically a very stressful and destructive process, she worked side-by-side with me to preserve our friendship. We ensured that, although our marriage was ending, our friendship remained intact.

One of the many ways Dalelynn directly impacted me was through her unwavering faith in my ability to succeed. I don't know what she saw in me, but she constantly encouraged and supported me in my passions and dreams as a DJ. At the time, I was a struggling hobbyist DJing on the side while working a dead-end job. Despite making less than $30,000 a year, DJing for pennies on the dollar wherever I could, she pushed me to take my passion seriously. She almost forced me to put systems in place, structure my processes, create contracts, and develop my website.

Her encouragement and belief in me transformed my life. In less than a year, I went from making a meager income to generating multiple six figures. We expanded, hiring multiple DJs, and eventually developed into a full-fledged wedding entertainment business. Honestly, without her, I'd probably still be fumbling with my mixtapes in my mom's basement, oblivious to the concept of 'business' and thinking I was living the dream.

Dalelynn's influence on my life has been profound. She exemplifies resilience emotionally, spiritually, and physically. Her journey has shown me that with faith, perseverance, and grace, we can overcome any challenge life throws our way. Through her example, I've learned to navigate adversity and remain steadfast in my purpose, making a positive difference in the world around me.

One significant way Dalelynn influenced me was through her faith in my abilities as a parent. Raising five children is no small feat, and she managed to do so with immense love and dedication. Observing her parenting style, I learned the importance of patience, understanding, and the power of leading by example. She showed me that being a parent is not just about providing for your children, but also about nurturing their dreams, encouraging their aspirations, and being their biggest supporter. Her strength and compassion have made me a better father, and I strive to emulate her dedication in my relationship with our children.

Additionally, Dalelynn was a pillar of support during one of the darkest periods of my life. I fell into a deep depression, feeling lost and overwhelmed by the challenges I faced. It was Dalelynn who recognized the signs and encouraged me to seek help, even when I was reluctant. She stood by me, offering unwavering support and reassurance. Her encouragement to seek professional help was a turning point for me. I learned that seeking help is not a sign of weakness, but rather a step towards healing and becoming stronger. Without her support and encouragement, I might still be trapped in that dark place.

Dalelynn's impact extended beyond our personal lives and into our professional relationship. When we decided to part ways as a married couple, we made a conscious effort to maintain a strong and positive co-parenting relationship. Her ability to put aside personal differences for the sake of our children was a testament to her character. We worked together to ensure that our children felt loved and supported, despite the changes in our family structure. This collaborative approach to co-parenting has not only benefited our children but also strengthened our friendship.

Another aspect of Dalelynn's influence was her entrepreneurial spirit. She had an innate ability to identify opportunities and turn them into successful ventures. Watching her navigate the world of business with confidence and determination was inspiring. She encouraged me to take risks, think outside the box, and pursue my passions with the same level of dedication. Her entrepreneurial mindset rubbed off on me, and I began to see the potential in my own ventures. Her success in various businesses served as a blueprint for my own journey, and I owe much of my professional growth to her guidance and example.

Dalelynn's journey of overcoming personal challenges has also been a source of inspiration. Her battle with obesity and her determination to lead a healthier lifestyle were nothing short of extraordinary. She transformed not only her physical appearance but also her mental and emotional well-being. Her story of weight loss and personal transformation was featured in People Magazine, highlighting her incredible achievements. This public recognition was a testament to her hard work and dedication, and it motivated me to strive for my own personal goals.

Moreover, Dalelynn's faith has been a cornerstone of her life, and it has profoundly influenced mine. Her unwavering belief in a higher power and her commitment to her faith have provided her with strength and resilience in the face of adversity. She has shown me the importance of faith and spirituality in navigating life's challenges. Through her example, I have learned to lean on my faith during difficult times and to find solace in prayer and worship. Her spiritual guidance has been a beacon of light in my life, helping me to stay grounded and focused on my purpose.

Dalelynn's ability to connect with people and inspire them is another remarkable trait. Whether through her work as a worship leader, her mission trips, or her business endeavors, she has touched the lives of countless individuals. Her genuine care for others and her desire to make a positive impact are qualities that I deeply admire. She has taught me the importance of giving back to the community and using my platform to inspire and uplift others. Her example has encouraged me to be more compassionate, empathetic, and proactive in making a difference in the lives of those around me.

In conclusion, Dalelynn Settle's influence on my life has been profound and multifaceted. She has shaped me into the person I am today through her resilience, faith, entrepreneurial spirit, and unwavering support. Her impact has been felt in my personal, professional, and spiritual life. Her journey of overcoming adversity and her dedication to helping others have inspired me to strive for greatness and to make a positive difference in the world. Dalelynn's story is a testament to the power of influence and the remarkable impact one person can have on another's life. Her strength and determination continue to inspire me and many others to push through our struggles and strive for greatness, no matter the odds.

ABOUT THE AUTHOR:

Social Media:
LinkedIn linkedin.com/in/david-settle-a5770748
Facebook facebook.com/thedavidsettle
Email dave@thedavidsettle.com

David Settle is an award-winning DJ, radio host, celebrity photographer, educator, entrepreneurial enthusiast, and proud parent of five. While studying music production, Christianity, and entrepreneurship in college, he launched his first successful business, DJS Entertainment, which quickly became one of Houston's premier wedding production companies. David holds a master's degree in entertainment business, further enriching his extensive expertise in the entertainment industry.

He cherishes his family, music, photography, creating compelling content, and witnessing God's transformative work!

David's unconventional upbringing on the streets of southwest Houston, TX, coupled with extensive experience in corporate America and church culture, uniquely inform his approach to business, family life, faith, and overall worldview.

KIRKPATRICK LOVE
Derrick Pearson

No one influences us like family. Our introduction to authentic love, real love, comes from those who love deepest. Family can be by blood, circumstance, chemistry, or love. I am blessed to be loved by many families and family types. There is one family who has shown me a different, special kind of love. This family is special. I will say this again so that it lands: This family is SPECIAL.

From its elders leading through humane and humble love through generations to its youngest, brightest, most brilliant members, this family is unique and authentic in the way that it loves, grows, and shines. Oxford defines special as "better, greater, or otherwise different from what is usual." Each member of this family will say that they are not any of those things, but I assure you that they are that in full. Each member is its own kind of special, allowing the unit to be special in how they work together, love together, and live together. There is an emotional dance within them that asks for love to be the first thing—the important thing. The family has several names as all families do, and each one has its own power, purpose, and way. They all connect in a perfect maze of excellence and love.

My introduction to the lady of this family was on a Saturday morning in the kitchen of her home. We were introduced and held hands almost immediately. We shared a smile and a hug, then proceeded to pick one another's brain and seek the other's heart. We shared jokes and curiosity and found ourselves constantly touching hands to stay connected. She was a lifelong educator, woman of faith, and good heart. She apologized too often for kindnesses I should have been thanking her for. She should have known how many times she asked exactly the right question to receive exactly the right answer.

MoVal (Mother Valerie) was a collection of wonderful lessons and missions. She moved and talked quietly unless she was playing piano and singing songs of faith. Her laugh often outsized her body, and her eyes had much greater vision than her tiny spectacles should have been able to process. Her faith allowed her balance and strength to love, and her ability to see and seek love was invigorating. She would listen, and in that talent was a part of her vibrancy. She received information that others might miss. She participated in conversations to learn. She sought more information directly from sources with real knowledge. She was constantly learning. She was constantly teaching.

"A great teacher gets taught while teaching" – Valerie

She wrote a poem when she was younger, "Where is my water fountain?" She lived in a time where people of color couldn't drink from white water fountains. She saw people of color not being able to vote or watch movies in certain theaters. She saw friction over buses and schools. She saw an injustice and did what others should have but wouldn't. It moved her to question the existence of unnecessary pain and to call for some resolution to it. Why does this exist? Is it necessary? What is my responsibility? Can I make it better? I must make it better.

She taught children of color, children in need, and adults who were curious. She taught faith, raised the children of other parents, and educated communities everywhere she went. She was a teacher, educator, and Mother Valerie. Angels on earth really do exist. She was an angel on this earth and turned any engagement with a human into a better existence.

I met the man of this family soon after. He was a standard setter and North Star. In his orbit, I felt small but gigantic next to him. I wanted to be his size, with his influence and power. I loved being in his gravitational pull. His voice was filled with command and volume, and he made a point to make sure that not only did he see me, but that I saw him. Not only did I hear him, but he heard me. His conversational rhythm was entirely required. He wanted to digest what you served him. He needed to know that you were receiving the goodness he was serving up. He was a master and a servant. He was gentle and robust. He was present and a presence. He spoke with calmness and purpose. He also reached out to touch often, almost to reassure me and himself of both realities. He was a leader through and through, and my soul told me that I should follow him. I have never been more right in my life. He shared his love of games and the people who played them. He pointed out that it was the people who mattered most and that the outcome was more important than the income.

That man was a wrecking ball of positive change and influence. He gave, he shared, and he impacted all things in his universe in a positive way with a positive result. He was also a DUDE. I remember watching him among his military peers and seeing the youthful energy emerge and shine. I listened to story after story of lessons and victories, highlighted by the elevating of how the victories were won and what the person went through to achieve them. He celebrated both the victory and the lesson. He needed to do so. I celebrate his victories and lessons.

When he became ill later in life, he sat in his bed and gave me yet another gift. He gave me his presence in my life forever in his voice and his manner. He went outside of his pain to provide some love to his son-in-law. He said something that moves me daily. I am forever in awe of his giving this life GPS to me.

"If you ever get lonely and need me, look forward and up. That's where I will be. That's where love is."

There was a brother that I met later, and I have to say that I am forever in awe of his poise. His brilliant mind and adventurous spirit provide wonderful joy whenever he is near. His thoughtfulness and consideration validate the desire to be closer to him. It is his writing that moved me closer to writing this myself. An incredible financial mind and his connection to nature make me wish I could meet him in those places at his level. It is his level alone. I am only meant to ponder what it would be like to meet him there.

There is a calm to the brother that inspires me to move in my own calm. His balanced approach to life requires that those in his space calm with him, for him, by him. He has this nature about him that is so wonderfully connected to the land around him that grounded makes more sense to me now. He is the compass to nature and all of its beauty. His eyes know things that my eyes envy. He goes to corners and heights that my fear won't allow. It is joyful to know that someone can. He is absolutely that someone.

There is added joy in his beautiful bride and partner. She is another educator and brilliant heart. To have the kind of heart that seeks out sharing the good parts of her soul makes her extremely balanced and strong. She climbs and marches and pushes through and up on paths and trails that most of us would buckle on. I admire her gifts. It appears that nature and the universe do as well. Natural has a greater meaning because of her. Her ability to connect with all is impressive. Brilliant even.

Caroline was a friend before we met, or so it seems. She roots for me and us, and it makes me look forward to being worthy of her cheering. She has seen and experienced so many wonderful moments, and her recall makes each lesson new and beautiful. She teaches life in the exact special kindness that she lives it. Naturally, purposefully, and beautifully.

This amazing couple did what amazing couples do. They created an amazing, world-conquering son to change the world beyond them. It is always remarkable to find a young person in this day and age who possesses today's technological mind and yesterday's old soul. To find a young person who not only cares about the planet but loves to engage it at its rawest level. He ponders and considers with such brilliance that I think he often catches himself off guard at how quickly the answers come to him. Cause and effect as a functional humanity. If he ever figures out how exceptional he is as a person, the world will be better for it.

I look forward to the young prince and his lifeline of wonderful things built and created. He will change the thoughts and actions of all who cross his path. He will elevate his space, his community, and honor the wonderful love poured into him by his family. There is a picture of a young prince on the side of a rock. He is alone but has allowed us to watch his excellence from below. We stand in awe of his ability to propel above us, all knowing that he will return to us mortals with wonderful stories of the space he ascended to. He will tell us how, and we will marvel at him.

Not to mention the wonderful Uncle Chip and his wife Mary, their incredible children and grandchildren, and various cousins would be disrespectful. This tree branch of excellence, love, and character has made my life a constant learning experience. I am always greater immediately when engaging them. They have such remarkable journeys and stories that I am always smarter after I have been loved by them. From shared moments with them in full or independently, I am better from their acceptance and purposeful goodness.

This incredible band of extraordinary people has another thing in common. They brought me the love of my life. The most intelligent person I have ever met is the daughter, sister, sister-in-law, and aunt of the family above. I am still not sure that I belong with these superhumans, but they sure seem to be okay with me being one of them.

On a late summer evening, I was invited to a party in Falls Church, Virginia. In a beautiful, cozy house covered in trees, I walked in and found my way to a beverage. I remember paying attention to who was at this party. I was invited by a friend who knew the host but had not met them. I immediately got caught up in the music and started dancing by myself. There, I noticed this sparkling smile standing there watching me. I asked who she was and was told that she was the host. It was her party. I almost immediately went over and asked her to dance. She said no. "I can't dance."

I had some strange self-imposed rules for dating back in the day. One such rule was that I could never seriously date anyone who could not dance. She had just told me the one thing that normally would make me run. "What do you mean you don't dance? Everyone dances." She then corrected and pivoted. "I can't dance the way YOU dance." Ah. That, I understood. This was the early 80s and I was in my hip-hop, pop-and-lock phase. Throw in some THRILLER DANCE and I pretty much was a Tasmanian devil on the dance floor. It wasn't exactly conducive to getting to know someone while I was doing it.

I begged her to dance, she smiled, and off we went. We danced and talked most of the night. I never recovered from her smile. In those days, it was common to dress up and go to Georgetown, which was in DC and had blocks of any and every kind of bar and nightclub you desired. I asked her if she would go dancing with me, and she decided to take me up on it as long as it was her friends and my friends.

I remember this vividly: we met at the bar. It was a bar where I knew everyone, and they knew me. What sticks in my mind was not worrying about anyone knowing I was with her. All my dance partners knew. Previous dance partners knew. Potential dance partners knew. And it mattered. I wanted them to know. It was then that I realized the peace of it all. That's how it was supposed to be. I wasn't supposed to care about anyone else in the bar. Wow.

It's almost four decades later and life has taught me several things. Captain America and his amazing wife were real. You can love your in-laws and it's really cool when they love you in return. There is nothing to be afraid of in love. Forever is a mighty long time.

I have been blessed with this family's love and presence. They work and live at such a high level of success that I have to elevate and progress to meet them there. I am thankful for them. I am thankful for her. I am thankful for their love.

ABOUT THE AUTHOR:

Social Media:

LinkedIn linkedin.com/in/derrick-pearson-b5580524/

Facebook facebook.com/derrick.pearson.5

Email pearsonderrick@aol.com

Derrick Pearson- Sports Radio Station Owner KNTK-FM Lincoln, Nebraska. 93.7 The Ticket FM. Host "Old School with Jay Foreman" "DP One on One" at 93.7 The Ticket FM Lincoln, Nebraska. Speaker-TEDxLander May 2019. The love Project Speaker-TEDxDeerPark March 2020. An American Face 11X Amazon Best Selling Author "The Impact of Influence, (Volumes 1-6) Rebuilt Through Recovery Black Man Love, Concrete Connections, and The Winning Mindset.

Derrick "DP" Pearson Sportscaster, radio and television host, writer, sports executive, and high school coach. That career has taken him nationwide, including Washington, DC, Charlotte, Los Angeles, Salt Lake City, Atlanta, and now Lincoln where he calls home. In addition to his media and coaching ventures, he also helped establish Fat Guy Charities in Charlotte, an NFL Charity, and developed LovePrints, a national mentor program that promotes Loving and Learning through Sports. DP joins Jay Foreman every weekday from 4pm to 6pm.

THE IMPORTANCE OF INTEGRITY AND KEEPING YOUR WORD: LESSONS LEARNED FROM LIFE'S ENCOUNTERS

Fendi Onobun

In my lifetime, I've experienced many lessons and encounters with various individuals and situations that have shaped who I am today. These moments serve as guideposts, illuminating the path we tread and the values we hold dear. Among the many lessons life imparts, few are as significant as the importance of being a person of your word. Through personal encounters and reflections, I have come to truly understand the profound significance of these principles and their impact on relationships, personal growth, and accountability.

During the COVID-19 pandemic, a time of global uncertainty and fear, I found myself seeking stability amidst the chaos. It was during this period that I encountered a real estate guru online, whose teachings resonated with my aspirations for financial prosperity and personal fulfillment.

The allure of real estate has always held a magnetic pull for me. Beyond the tangible assets, I saw it as a conduit for building wealth and leaving a lasting legacy for my family. While the world was in turmoil, the opportunity presented itself to learn from a seasoned expert in the field. I eagerly purchased his courses, looking to gain insights and wisdom from his program.

What made this experience even more exciting was discovering a mutual acquaintance between the guru and myself. In a world governed by connections and networks, this shared bond created a sense of familiarity and trust for me. I vividly recall expressing my admiration for his teachings and my eagerness to embark on the journey of real estate entrepreneurship. In response, the guru extended an offer of mentorship and told me to contact him anytime for guidance through the intricacies of the industry. With a shared vision and a mutual friend as a bridge, I looked forward to the possibilities. I contacted the guru as soon as I completed his program so we could get started on a game plan.

After I completed his program, I reached out to him several times, until I realized he wasn't going to respond. It was all just talk. Yet, as the adage goes, actions speak louder than words, and his promises fell short of expectations. The guru, whose guidance I had eagerly sought, ghosted me. This disillusionment served as a reminder of the importance of integrity and character. The guru didn't owe me anything, but the breach of trust still stung. It underscored the inherent value of one's word. For me, being a person of your word has become a non-negotiable. It forms credibility, serving as a compass while navigating life's complexities. The incident with the real estate guru reinforced the importance of doing what you say you're going to do and prompted introspection of my commitment to upholding my own words.

Reflecting on this, I am reminded of a quote that sums up my experience with the guru: "People with good intentions make promises; people with good character keep them." - Unknown

The incident with the real estate guru highlighted the significance of communication in fostering trust. Sometimes, things happen where an individual may not be able to do what they said they would, or people just flat out forget, or overcommit. In that case, have the respect and decency to communicate that. Don't just ghost the person, take some personal responsibility and communicate that you aren't able to do what you said you would and move on. I have no problem with that.

I remember an encounter I had with a homeless man that left an impression on me, and If I'm being honest, it was my experience with the guru that influenced my actions in this moment. I was on my way to an appointment in downtown Houston, running a little late. Amidst the hustle and bustle of downtown traffic, I was stopped at a red light. As I waited for the light to turn green, a homeless man approached my driver-side window. He said, "Hey man, I don't mean no harm. I just wanted to ask if you could buy me some food at this McDonald's down the street."

I found myself torn between the demands of time and the call of compassion. His simple request for sustenance echoed the cries of countless marginalized individuals I frequently see in downtown Houston. Despite the constraints of time and obligation, I made a promise to the man that I'd return after my appointment and get him some food at McDonald's.

Some might view such gestures as inconsequential, fleeting moments of altruism amidst daily life. For me, it was a testament to the power of integrity and the fulfillment of promises. It reaffirmed my belief that small acts of kindness have the potential to ignite hope and restore faith in humanity. It was also a reaffirmation to be true to my word. After my appointment, I returned to the intersection to look for the homeless man. There, next to a parking garage, I found him.

"Hey, you still want that McDonald's?" I asked him. His eyes looked at me with skepticism. "I told you I'd come back." His demeanor softened, and we walked to McDonald's together. I invited him to order whatever he wanted. His modest request for a hotcakes and sausage meal underscored the humility and gratitude that often accompany moments of vulnerability. In that moment, I was reminded of the inherent dignity and worth of every individual.

My encounter with the homeless man served as a powerful reminder of the impact compassion and integrity can have. It reinforced my belief that the fulfillment of promises, no matter how seemingly insignificant, has the potential to catalyze positive change and foster genuine human connection.

In essence, integrity is not merely a virtue to be upheld; it is a way of being, a guiding principle that informs our actions and shapes our character. It is a commitment to authenticity, transparency, and accountability. These qualities serve as pillars of trust and credibility in both personal and professional spheres. Integrity extends beyond individual interactions; it is the cornerstone of a just and equitable society. In a world plagued by distrust and division, the fulfillment of integrity and unity serve as a beacon of hope and fosters a sense of promise.

Experiences like these have led me to inspire others through my C.O.R.E. principles, an acronym I often speak about that compels me to make a positive difference in our world. Let us strive to be individuals of integrity, whose words are synonymous with action, so that we can continue the good work of humanity and impact those around us for a better tomorrow.

ABOUT THE AUTHOR:

Social Media:
Facebook facebook.com/FendiOnobun
Email info@fendispeaks.org

Fendi Onobun is a former NFL tight end and two-sport collegiate athlete who enjoyed a five-year career with the St. Louis Rams, Buffalo Bills, and Jacksonville Jaguars. In 2015, Onobun suffered a career-ending knee injury that abruptly altered his path, prompting him to redirect his focus back to his roots in Houston, Texas.

Returning to his hometown, Onobun didn't let adversity define him; instead, he embraced it as an opportunity to make a lasting impact on his community. Through philanthropy, entrepreneurship, and writing, Fendi has become a beacon of hope and inspiration for countless individuals, especially the youth. Onobun's dedication to giving back is evident in his commitment to hosting free football camps, organizing community drives, and hosting speaking engagements aimed at empowering young people to pursue their dreams relentlessly.

In 2018, Onobun added "published author" to his list of accomplishments with the release of his debut book, "Transition: One Kid's Bank Shot to the NFL." This work serves as a testament to the power of perseverance, hard work, and unwavering faith. Through his writing, Onobun seeks to inspire others to overcome obstacles and pursue their passions with determination.

In 2023, Onobun expanded his philanthropic efforts by establishing the C.O.R.E. Leadership Foundation, a non-profit organization dedicated to supporting students in underserved communities. Through a variety of programs, workshops, and resources, the foundation empowers young individuals with the tools they need to achieve success and unlock their full potential.

Beyond his professional pursuits, Onobun is a devoted family man, cherishing his role as a father to two boys, Fendi II and Prince, and a loving husband to his wife Stephanie. His ability to balance his personal and professional life while remaining deeply rooted in his community speaks volumes about his character and values.

Fendi Onobun's accomplishments serve as a reminder that setbacks are merely stepping stones on the path to success and that true greatness lies in one's ability to uplift others and make a positive impact on the world.

TWO NICKELS
JD Hurd

What is influence? The Oxford Dictionary defines it as "the capacity to have an effect on the character, development, or behavior of someone or something, or the effect itself." The greatest influence in my life did not come from a person but from a state of being: poverty. The psychological influence of poverty on my life was real and profound.

If you let it, poverty can either break you or make you. The psychological impact of poverty often causes a person to question their value in this world. Take my childhood, for example. I primarily grew up in the projects, low-rent apartments for those who cannot afford housing without government assistance. Unfortunately, what was meant to aid the less fortunate was often turned into something negative by a few bad actors.

The projects I grew up in were named Bessemer Projects, located in a small city in Alabama called Prichard. Like most project communities, Bessemer Projects were often plagued by drugs, gangs, and prostitution, among other things. Growing up there was challenging. You might think that all my days in the projects were difficult, but that wasn't always the case. I did have some good times, but make no mistake—it was still a perilous place to live.

The Realization of Being Poor

I can recall the day I realized I was poor. I was in the eighth grade at K.J. Clark Middle School. There was a Burger King on the corner, up the street from the school. You could smell the chargrilled food that Burger King restaurants emit. One day after football practice, my friends and I decided to stop at Burger King before walking home. Back then, Burger King had a special: two Whoppers for a dollar (a dollar and seven cents with tax). We all got dressed after practice and started to check how much money we had. I reached into my pocket and pulled out two nickels. That's right, ten cents! Then one of my good friends had a field day making fun of me because I only had two nickels. That was the day I realized I was poor. I did not have a concept of money until that day. No one shared their Whoppers with me. I walked home hungry and embarrassed after watching my friends devour every bit of their Whoppers. It was that day I decided to do my best never to be poor when I grew up. The psychological impact of poverty went on to influence my life both negatively and positively.

The Negative Impact

Poverty dealt a major blow to my self-worth as a child. It has a way of making you think that you have no value to add and that you are worth nothing. You might ask, how so? Let us go back to the two nickels. Just understand that I was not given those two nickels— I had found them. My mother was not in a financial position to give me money. We weren't even in a position to have lunch money; we were in the free and reduced lunch program. As a kid, I wondered why I did not have enough money like the other kids to buy a Whopper. Why were they better than me? Being poor took me there as a kid, wondering if these other kids were better than me because they had material things. They had designer clothes and shoes, their parents had brand new cars, and they lived in houses instead of the projects.

As a result of feeling like a second-class citizen, I became shy and introverted in many ways. I stayed up under my mama because she was like my security blanket. I had to belong to something to feel like I was worth something. I became driven to play sports because it made me feel like I was worth something. Poverty made me very guarded as a kid. When I should have been having fun doing an activity, I was wondering if I measured up. We could have just been playing something as simple as marbles, and I couldn't enjoy it because I was focused on whether I measured up. I couldn't even enjoy being an incredible athlete; I was too worried about what someone would think of me because I lived in the projects. Man, that was tough. The negative impact of poverty pulled the fun out of many things for me as a kid.

The negative impact of poverty on me as an adult was that it influenced me to be driven to be successful for all the wrong reasons. You might ask, how so? My definition of success as a young adult was to have pretty women, lots of money, and be the CEO of a major corporation. Let's talk about having pretty women. Lord have mercy! Being shallow was a direct by-product of poverty for me. Let me be clear. All women are beautiful, and it has nothing to do with their physical looks. But when you degrade your value, then you will degrade the value of other people. Poverty influenced me to chase that all-mighty dollar. I spent a great part of my professional career trying to amass money, power, and status, often at the expense of my family. I thought giving my wife and kids all the material things I didn't have as a child would show them that I loved them. Oh, how mistaken I was. The number one way you show your family that you love them is to spend time with them.

I recall when I lived in Dallas, Texas. I would travel to Austin, Houston, San Antonio, Brownsville, McAllen, Denver, Charlotte, and New York. Many times, I would leave on a Sunday and not return home until Thursday. I had a misconception that traveling as a professional gave you a certain elite status. Don't get me wrong, I made an exceptionally good living in corporate America, and it afforded my family all that I never could have even imagined as a child. But when it boiled down to it, I was driven to climb the corporate ladder because I didn't want to be poor like I was as a child, and I realized providing for my family was the secondary reason. In a nutshell, my family was second to my work. You may say there is nothing wrong with wanting to excel professionally. Well, my question to you is, at what expense? Certainly not at the expense of your family. The negative influence of poverty will cause one to lose the need for balance in life. It certainly happened to me.

The Positive Impact

You have seen the negative impact of poverty on my life as a child and as a young adult. But there is always a yin to the yang. Poverty also had a positive effect on my life. One, it made me close to my mom and obedient. As hard as my mom was working to keep food in our mouths and clothes on our backs, even if they were hand-me-downs, and a roof over our heads, even if it was in the projects, I had tremendous respect and love for her sacrifices. I was not going to be disrespectful as a child or as an adult to my mom. She had it hard enough already.

The other positive influence poverty had on my life was that it drove me to embrace the church. Yes, my mom made us go to church when we were kids, like a lot of other parents. However, I did not start to realize that I was worth something until I started paying attention in church. Oh, you better believe that when I started paying attention in church, the questions started to flow from my mind to God. The number one question I had was why I had to be poor. The second question was why I had to die to be rich. Well, I got my answers. First, I did not have to be poor, and secondly, I did not have to die to be rich. Wow! What a total misunderstanding of the Bible. Thank God for the sisters at Andrew Street Church of Christ in Mobile, Alabama. Some of them have passed away, and many have moved to other parts of the country. However, as a youth, they instilled in me the foundation that put me on the right path as a seasoned adult. The late Sister Boroughs, the late Sister Holt, Sister

Bernice Powell, and Sister Jackie Powell. They taught me the scriptures backward and forward. They taught me that I had to be baptized for the remission of my sins according to the scriptures (Acts 2:38), that I was worth something, and that God had a purpose for me in my lifetime. You may say, here we go again with that church stuff. Well, you must do you, and I have to do me, but we both must do right. The lessons they taught me are what brought me out of a downward spiral in life.

I partied in college like a lot of young adults. My drink was Mad Dog 20/20 Orange Jubilee, and that Jubilee had nothing to do with church either. I recall one time my friend and I were so drunk that we both were sleeping in the car at a stoplight in Northport, Alabama, with the car just burning out because my friend's foot was on the gas and thankfully on the brakes at the same time. We should have been dead that night or, at the very least, locked up in jail. When I was a young professional, I partied and did everything under the sun. Once again, that drink got the best of me. When I lived in the Dallas-Fort Worth area, one time I traveled from deep in Dallas back to my apartment in Garland, Texas, and I couldn't even tell you how I got home. Once again, I should have been dead or in jail. Those incidents made me realize something: I was still poor, not materially, but spiritually. One of the lessons those sisters instilled in me was to turn to God, and you will find that He was facing you the whole time. What are you talking about, Coach Hurd? Back to the two nickels. What I realized was that God wanted me to understand those two nickels were worth five cents each, and five plus five equals ten. You are a perfect ten. Now add a zero to that ten and keep it one hundred.

ABOUT THE AUTHOR:

Social Media:

LinkedIn linkedin.com/in/jd-hurd-msl-usatf-ustfccca-810742b7

Facebook facebook.com/coachhurd32

Email jdhurd32@gmail.com

JD Hurd is the Head Boys Track and Cross-Country Coach at Conroe High School. He helps student-athletes and adults alike reach their goals in life by providing rock-solid guidance.

Before starting his coaching and teaching career in the public school system, Coach Hurd spent 18 years as a Retirement Specialist and Wealth Management Advisor in the financial services industry while also directing a junior Olympic youth track club. After a successful career helping individuals reach their financial goals and guiding young athletes to the Junior Olympics, Coach Hurd now focuses on helping student-athletes and adults build the necessary foundation to be productive citizens.

Coach Hurd holds a Bachelor of Science in Business with a concentration in Corporate Finance and Investment Management from the University of Alabama and a Master of Science in Leadership from Walden University. He also holds track and cross-country certifications from the United States Association of Track and Field and the United States Track and Field Cross Country Coaches Association.

Coach Hurd enjoys giving inspirational messages through his platform, "The Word from Coach Hurd," and watching movies with his wife and kids.

Coach Hurd is available as a motivational speaker. You can reach him at jdhurd32@gmail.com.

IGNITING A SPARK
Jose Escobar

There are a number of people who have left their mark on my life in immeasurable ways. Each of them has enhanced my life in a unique and lasting way. For this chapter, I'd like to focus on the late Dr. Lennard George and his wife, Dr. Arlene George. In the early 2000s, I joined Amway (formerly known as Quixtar), a network marketing company, as a young, bright-eyed entrepreneur. I was eager and excited to take on the world. Under the tutelage of Drs. Lennard and Arlene, I developed a bigger vision for what I wanted out of life and began to dream bigger than I ever thought I would.

Drs. Lennard and Arlene were both busy professionals, practicing physicians with three young children when we first met. They knew they wanted more out of life in pursuit of financial independence. This is what drew them to join Amway, where they built a successful business. At some point along their journey, they recruited me onto their team. It was during this time in my life that I first immersed myself in personal development by reading books, attending seminars, and listening to tapes (which eventually turned into CDs). We would attend weekly meetings in Bowie, Maryland, where successful entrepreneurs would "share the plan" by presenting the business opportunity to new guests. Once this meeting ended, all the IBOs (independent business owners) would stay behind for extra training. I absolutely loved being surrounded by successful dreamers. The conviction and passion in the room were palpable. The meetings would end with everyone making a circular motion with their fist in the air while chanting, "oooooo, flush that stinkin' job, woooooo!" (The collective goal of most people in Amway was to build a side home-based business that would ultimately enable them to leave their day job.) One of the best parts of these nights was the meeting after the meeting, called the "Night Owl." Only the serious leaders were encouraged to attend these meetings in a local restaurant or someone's home. These night owls would often go on for hours. These were some of the most influential and formative moments in my life. I had people on my sidelines who were in the trenches with me, working hard on their side businesses to make a better life for themselves and their families. There was something special about these people and those rooms during those times. We laughed and cried together, shared personal stories and dreams, and were always there for each other during the good, the bad, and the ugly.

The stickiness behind the scenes that connected me to my business and Amway was Drs. Lennard and Arlene. There were a couple of years when I felt like I spent more time with them than I did with some of my best friends. We traveled the roads together, driving from state to state for seminars, boot camps, and conventions. We shared hotel rooms, broke bread together, and inspired each other at every opportunity. Many times, we had game planning sessions at their house on how we would get to diamond status in Amway. We aspired to build massive teams and change lives for the better. We would pull out whiteboards and map out strategic plans, listing names of potential recruits on sheets of paper. There was tons of training that we would invite team members to attend.

The fact that Drs. Lennard and Arlene would take their valuable spare and non-productive time (which was limited) and pour into me and many others in pursuit of building a home-based business spoke volumes about not only the quality of Amway but also the caliber of people they were. I can recall many times when Dr. Lennard would sit me down, man to man, and pour into me with his wisdom. He would pull a book, such as The Man of Steel and Velvet by Aubrey P. Andelin or Tender Warrior by Stu Weber, and of course, The Magic of Thinking Big by David J. Schwartz, just to name a few. He would say, "Jose, I need you to read these books, and I want you to come back to me when you're done and tell me how you are going to implement what you learn in your life." He was becoming more than just my coach in business; he was becoming a mentor and friend. Dr. Arlene would always inquire about my relationships with family and friends. She would always give me her insights on the importance of treating women with dignity and respect at the highest level. There are so many golden nuggets that I learned over the years, not only from what they said to me but from what I witnessed in how they lived their lives. It's been said, "Your actions speak so loudly, I hear not what you say." Truth be told, if they never said a word to me, I could just watch how they lived their lives, and that example was more than worth modeling. Dr. Lennard always treated his wife with so much kindness and respect at all times. I saw how he adored her and was always willing to go out of his way to remind her of that. Dr. Arlene equally was graceful in how she honored and served her husband. She would always speak highly of him and was always there for anything that was needed. They were an absolute power couple. There were many times on road trips and at different events where things might not have gone smoothly or as planned, and they would always meet the challenges head-on with a smile on their faces.

I've got to say, as a result of their mentorship and leadership over the years, I stepped into the entrepreneurial shoes with excellence at a young age. My family members were always saying how positive I was and how I inspired them to be more, do more, and have more. There were times when one of my older brothers would jokingly say to me, "Man, I feel like you're getting brainwashed." I would laughingly reply, "I think we could all use some positive brainwashing." There is something to be said about the power of pursuing personal development and desiring to pursue one's best self. One of the richest places you'll find in society today that is completely underutilized and overlooked is the self-help section in bookstores. Every book you will find in that section has years of experience crammed into a read you can devour in a few hours. So accessible, and many would consider it low-hanging fruit, yet many people do not take advantage of what's right under their noses. Drs. Lennard and Arlene instilled in me an insatiable thirst for reading, dreaming big dreams, and believing it's possible to achieve anything I set my mind to. I could go on and on about how they have abundantly impacted and influenced my life.

We did some really cool things together during those wonderful years in Amway. We impacted many lives in a positive way and made some good money simultaneously. We got to rub shoulders with millionaires and learn from some of the best in business, including people like Bill Britt (founder of Britt Worldwide), Paul Miller, Chris Cherest, and many others. Sadly, the journey with Amway came to a screeching halt when my dear friend and mentor (who ultimately became like a brother to me), Dr. Lennard George, passed away from a brain tumor in a very unexpected way on April 21, 2005. I remember feeling like I lost a brother, and I was in complete shock. Words cannot explain how hard it was to see his family go through this traumatic time and to witness all the family and friends that were devastated. I shed many tears, and it took a while to accept his passing. We always got along so well, and it's no surprise given that we were both Aquariuses and shared the exact same birthday of January 25th. Every year, to this day, on my actual birthday, I always say a special prayer for Dr. Lennard George. He will forever be loved and missed and hold a special place in my heart. His legacy lives on through his amazing wife, Dr. Arlene George, and their three wonderful children who are now grown and pursuing their dreams. I am forever grateful and blessed to have had so many cherished memories over the years with the George family.

As a result of the guidance, love, and support I received from both Drs. Lennard and Arlene, I can easily say this has directly played a role in the success I have today. From the early days at

Amway, I always had the dream of being the first millionaire in my entire family. I never lost sight of that goal and have kept my foot on the gas to this day. In honor of Dr. Lennard, I am overjoyed to say that I have officially hit seven figures in my business, making my goal come to life. My company, The Connected Leaders Academy, is all about bringing entrepreneurs together globally so we can all achieve more and create an impact in the lives of others. The exciting part is that this is just phase one of what I intend to do to make my dent in the world. As of this writing, The Connected Leaders Academy has four hundred paid members in forty-five states across the United States and twenty-one international countries. I am a fourteen-time, award-winning, bestselling published author. I have five different high-ticket programs and courses that I sell. I also have multiple live events that I host each year and a high-ticket mastermind, just to name a few of my ten income streams. Just to be clear, I don't say this to toot my own horn or impress anyone who's reading this. I say this to honor Drs. Lennard and Arlene for having poured into me, believed in me, and inspired me to go after my dreams.

Life is precious, and we live it fully one day at a time. As stated earlier, there are many people who have played a role in my achievements thus far, both personally and professionally. With that being said, there is no doubt that Drs. Lennard and Arlene deserve this recognition for the ripple effect they have created by pouring into me and others. We will never know how far their impact will go, but what I do know is that it is my responsibility to pay it forward. Over two decades later, I have finally flushed that stinkin' job after all, just not in the way I thought I would have (now a full-time entrepreneur as of January 2023). Sometimes in life, you don't know how things are going to play out. All you can do is control the controllables, such as habits, discipline, the people in your circle, use of spare and non-productive time, where you spend your money, and your attitude, just to name a few. Zig Ziglar said it best: "You were born to win, but to be a winner you must plan to win, prepare to win, and expect to win." My encouragement to you today is to go and win big in life. Start now. Start today. Your best is yet to come.

Thank you, Drs. Lennard and Arlene George, for igniting a spark in me that will never go out and will continue to impact the world for generations to come.

ABOUT THE AUTHOR:

Social Media:
LinkedIn linkedin.com/jaesco25
Facebook facebook.com/jaesco25/
Email jaesco25@gmail.com

Jose Escobar, an acclaimed personal development speaker and 14-time published author, leads two successful businesses: The Entrepreneur's Bookshelf and the Connected Leaders Academy, which has surpassed 7-figures in 15 months organically. He engages with entrepreneurs and advanced leaders, collectively reaching over 30 million people through presentations and coaching programs. He works with over 400 successful leaders globally. Jose is a master sales professional and is happily married with six kids. Discover more about Jose's offerings at
www.ConnectedLeadersAcademy.com.

A STORY OF COURAGE, HOPE AND PERSEVERANCE
Kenneth Morris

"Let those black guys fly!" – First Lady Eleanor Roosevelt referring to the Tuskegee Airmen, overheard by Mrs. Azellia White.

As a black pilot and Post-9/11 Navy Veteran with multiple medals, I have served as a combat aircrewman, recently including a historic VIP flight with the U.S. Navy Blue Angels and more. It is empowering and encouraging to learn of those who fought for the opportunity that allows me the privilege of doing what I do today - fly airplanes.

The story of Mrs. Azellia White is one that many have never heard, and even today, many are still unaware of it. For me personally, she is a true hero who exuded courageousness and accomplished feats decades ahead of her time that still resonate today! As a pioneering black woman pilot who lived to be 106 years old, she paved the way for many aviators, male and female. I am honored to have not only met her when she was a vibrant 103 years old on multiple occasions and gained her insight on life, flying, and being a good person, but also worked to get her inducted into the Texas Aviation Hall of Fame.

How did I come to meet Mrs. Azellia White? One day, I was sitting in my barber's chair on a typical Saturday, and like any other appointment with Ed, we would talk about family, sports, relationships, current news, etc. For a black man, the barbershop is often a place to feel like you can just be yourself, speak freely, and learn a thing or two that you had not known beforehand – it is a place of refuge. Ed, my barber for over 15 years, has never given me bad information nor negative energy, and that is one of the primary reasons he has been my barber for so long, besides giving great haircuts. So, as I was sitting in his chair on this particular Saturday, he made the statement, "Hey Ken, I know you are working at the Lone Star Flight museum now, and there is a lady across the street, Mrs. White, who I think worked in aviation and whose husband did something with airplanes many years ago. They used to have airplane parts in the garage that you can see when they lift the door, and I think you should go introduce yourself to see who they are. Also, she was cutting her own grass until she was 99 years old." Immediately, my interest was piqued, and I made it my business to find out who this mysterious couple living in South Park/Sunnyside, Texas – in what's considered the "hood" – were, having been involved in aviation for almost the last 100 years. I had no idea what I was getting into or that it would lead to various Aviation Hall of Fame inductions, as well as articles being written and video documentaries in the Washington Post, CNN, ABC, The Times, BET, and countless other news and media outlets around the world!

I attempted to visit Mrs. White on three separate occasions, but I was questioned by her very protective caretaker about why I needed to speak to her and if I was a reporter, which was understandable. On the fourth visit, when she noticed I was going to keep returning, she allowed me the opportunity to meet Mrs. White, and my entire life changed when she began telling me her story. I literally got goosebumps. I thought I was going there to learn about her husband, Hulon "Pappy" White, who is also a pioneer in his own right. Her husband was a famed Tuskegee Airman who worked as a master mechanic in Tuskegee. Azellia, who spent time in Tuskegee, decided that she wanted to become a pilot and saw it through, becoming the first black woman pilot in the state of Texas in 1946. Note: The legendary Bessie Coleman, the first black woman pilot, also from Texas, had to go to France to get her license (1926) because no one would teach her to fly in the US due to her being a black woman. Hulon "Pappy" White and Azellia White returned to Houston to create the first and only black airport on the south side of town that trained black people how to fly. Only a concrete slab currently remains from that historic endeavor.

Since my 18th birthday, I have been very fortunate to be introduced to aviation and the many facets it encompasses, as well as the people it brings together daily. My childhood was not filled with airports, exotic vacations, or anything that I can directly tie to what I am currently doing in life. The only constant highlight was attending Fred A. Lennon Youth Camp for four (4) summers straight in Magnolia, Texas, which was a great time. I have been blessed to meet many amazing people along the way, encounter great mentors, and have supportive friends, associates, and family, which has been key to much of the progress in my life.

My childhood did not afford me the luxury of dreaming about being a pilot or hopping onto an airplane and just leaving. I recall as a young boy in the 5th Ward, the sun beating down relentlessly on the cracked asphalt of the basketball courts, while I played from 7 am until nighttime to give myself something positive to do. "Swish! You can't hold me! You better go get some help!" I would yell as I made another basket repeatedly against my peers. I am not sure how or why, but basketball became a passion of mine early in life, and I was much better than the average child my age in my neighborhood. I was a skinny but wiry kid, set in determination as I practiced making 100 shots, layups, and pull-up jumpers repeatedly. Basketball was my escape from the harsh realities of life in the 5th Ward, and the NBA was going to be my way out and how I supported my family one day! That dream never came to reality.

For as long as I can remember, I started life with my grandmother Ninee, three sisters, Kristin, Kendra, Kathryn, my uncle Carl, my mother who would come and go, as well as Mr. DJ, my grandmother's late common-law husband. Our residence was a very small, 2-bedroom, 1-bath house just a few blocks from the train tracks, and it was usually loud and noisy. Money was always tight. I recall my grandmother cleaning wealthy white people's homes and getting paid daily just to keep a roof over our heads and food on the table. We did not have a car, so she would ride the Metro bus to and from work. I did not understand the value of money, how to get it, and definitely not how to budget it, but my grandmother made a way even in an environment plagued by crime, drugs, and violence. Gunshots rang out most nights, and sirens were a constant backdrop.

Despite the rough environment, I found solace on the basketball court and in school – S.A. Pleasants Elementary, Holland Middle School, St. Thomas High School, Nimitz High School, and ultimately graduating from Jesse H. Jones High School in the Houston Independent School District. I was a great student through middle school, but when I reached high school, I began looking at the world differently; my priorities shifted, and my focus pivoted to my own self-gratification and exploring who I thought I was.

After barely graduating high school, receiving no athletic or academic scholarships, and not wanting to work a dead-end job, I made a professional decision that would change the trajectory of my life forever – enlisting in the United States Navy to fly as a Combat Aircrewman searching for nuclear submarines around the world. It was the opportunity of a lifetime to become exposed to a world I never knew existed and never believed I could truly fit into – imposter syndrome is real even though I did not realize it at that time.

Basic training was grueling, both physically and mentally. After basic training, I went to Naval Aircrew Candidate School in Pensacola, Florida, then S.E.R.E. School (Survival, Evasion, Resistance, and Escape) in Brunswick, Maine, Rescue Swimmer training, and acoustic dissemination courses. I drew strength from my upbringing, from the lessons of perseverance and grit that had been instilled in me since childhood. I made it through, emerging as an Anti-Submarine Acoustic Warfare Systems Operator, a role that would take me to the far corners of the globe flying aboard the P-3C Orion aircraft. For the next several years, I sailed the world's oceans, monitoring sonar and radar systems to detect potential threats from submarines from China, Russia, North Korea, Pakistan, Iran, and many other countries. The Navy instilled in me a sense of discipline and purpose, qualities that would serve me well for the rest of my life.

After separating from the Navy with an honorable discharge, I found myself adrift, unsure of my next steps. I was honored to receive a basketball scholarship from Seward County College in Liberal, Kansas, thanks to All-American volleyball player and my cousin, Ashyn Carter. I earned my Associate of Science degree in Computer Information Systems with a 3.5 GPA and knew I had made the right career decision. However, I drifted from contract job to contract job, not feeling fulfilled, struggling with finances, and lacking the real spark to pursue anything truly challenging and meaningful in life. While in college, I visited the local regional airport, met with pilot instructors, and made a decision that I would re-join the industry that I cared so much about and ultimately become a pilot, even if it took me 10, 15 years – it took 20.

My journey in aviation is atypical. I began by flying in the Navy as an enlisted aircrewman, a job I am convinced was the best any 18-year-old could have. After leaving the Navy, I went to college, obtained my Associates degree, and resumed flying. Due to the high cost of becoming a pilot, my plans were placed on hold. In the meantime, I founded my own nonprofit, Universal Elite Aerospace, served as the Founding Director of Education for the new Lone Star Flight Museum in Houston, Texas, and later as the Executive Director of the Aviation Community Foundation. I left the museum when I was accepted into a prestigious new flying initiative called Forces to Flyers, funded by the U.S. Department of Transportation, which allowed veterans with aspirations to fly to obtain their pilot certificates and become commercial airline pilots. Additionally, I speak with K-12 students nationwide about the numerous rewarding opportunities in aviation, aerospace, and STEM industries, mentor junior enlisted servicemembers, new aviators, serve as a Board Member for STEM Flights, and Co-Chair for the National Business Aviation Association (NBAA) Endeavor Group.

It is because of Mrs. Azellia White that I am inspired to keep pushing, working hard, and providing hope to others who desire more out of life. Though Mrs. White has gained her eternal wings, there are others following in her footsteps whom I am very grateful to know personally. The lives and accomplishments of professional and groundbreaking pilots such as Theresa Claiborne, M'Lis Ward, Kimberly McCommon, Nia Wordlaw, Angel Hughes, Jessica Lafond, Tachiana Smith, Patricia Grisham, Zakiyah Percey, Kimberly Ford, Stephanie Davis, Anne-Marie Barry, Alexis Robinson, Khady Ndiaye Wooden, Mary Smith, Anya Kearns, Laura Humphries, Monique Grayson, Patrice Clark-Washington, Stephanie Grant, Diana Lugemwa, Tara Wright, Stephanie Hartsfield, June Marsh (Bronze Eagles), Jeanine Menze, La' Shanda Holmes, Ronaqua Russell, Nicole Sturrett, Nicole Alicea, Madeline Swegle, Carol Hopson, and many more need to be highlighted and celebrated as well.

Today, as I look back on the journey to where I am and the numerous obstacles that have come my way, one can't help but reflect on the long and winding road that has brought me to this point. From the basketball courts of the 5th Ward to the depths of the ocean as a Navy Acoustic Operator, from the challenges of veteran homelessness and depression to the heights of the clouds as a commercial pilot, this journey has been one of perseverance, resilience, and an unwavering belief in the power of believing in God, yourself, and never giving up, regardless of how difficult a current situation may appear.

Young people from the same neighborhoods where I grew up, once places of despair, are now soaring through the skies, their eyes alight with wonder and possibility. I watch with pride as they master the principles of flight, their minds expanding beyond the confines of their circumstances. It has been a dream come true – an opportunity to share my passion for aviation on a grander scale, to inspire and educate a new generation of pilots, engineers, and aviation enthusiasts. I pour myself into helping others, developing innovative educational programs and materials that bring the wonders of flight to inner-city kids who are typically unaware of all the possibilities afforded to them.

A strong sense of pride resides within me. After overcoming the odds and defying the expectations of those who had written me off from the start, and never affording me a fair chance, it was that energy that propelled me to strive and push even harder than I knew was possible. In doing so, I opened doors not just for myself but for countless others who dared to dream of a life exceeding anything they could have previously imagined.

I am living proof that no matter how dark the night, the dawn will always break – and with it, the promise of a new day, a new beginning, and the limitless possibilities that await those brave enough to spread their wings and take flight.

ABOUT THE AUTHOR:

Social Media:
LinkedIn linkedin.com/in/mrkennethmorris/
Facebook facebook.com/MrKennethMorris
Email sirkennethmorris@gmail.com

Kenneth Morris is a decorated United States Navy Veteran who flew aboard the P-3C Orion (now P-8 Poseidon) aircraft based at Naval Air Station Whidbey Island, Washington. As a Second Class Petty Officer, he worked as an Anti-Submarine Warfare Systems Operator - Acoustic Operator and earned qualification as an Enlisted Aviation Warfare Specialist. Kenneth served as an Operation Enduring Freedom/Operation Iraqi Freedom Veteran and received numerous awards and medals, including the Navy and Marine Corps Achievement Medal, NATO Medal, Kosovo Air Campaign Medal, Armed Forces Expeditionary Medal, Sea Service Deployment Medal, and more.

Born and raised in Houston, Texas, Kenneth is the oldest sibling to seven younger sisters. After separating with an Honorable discharge, he graduated from Seward County College in Liberal, Kansas with a 3.5 GPA and a degree in Computer Information Systems. Currently, he is completing a Bachelor of Business Administration in Management with a Minor in Innovation and Entrepreneurship at Prairie View A&M University.

Upon returning to Houston, Kenneth founded Universal Elite Aerospace in November 2013, an Aviation S.T.E.M. Outreach program that motivates and inspires youth and teens to excel in the aviation and aerospace sector. His organization positively engaged more than 50,000 youth, teens, and young adults in a 3-year span.

In December 2016, Kenneth was appointed Director of Education and Outreach for the new $40M Lone Star Flight Museum in Houston, Texas, where he developed aviation education, S.T.E.M. curriculum, and organized field trips for 1.2 million youth throughout the Greater Houston and Harris County area.

In December 2018, Kenneth successfully transitioned careers when he was selected as one of seven U.S. Military Veterans from a pool of thousands for a national flying initiative, 'Forces to Flyers', powered by the U.S. Department of Transportation. He was the only African American and minority chosen to participate in Texas under this new initiative.

From February 2020 to February 2024, Kenneth served as the Executive Director of the Aviation Community Foundation, where he continues to provide access to internship opportunities, scholarships, and more for students across the country aspiring to become the next generation of aviation professionals. His primary focus remains on increasing awareness of Diversity, Equity, Inclusion, and Leadership Accountability throughout the entire aviation and aerospace industry.

THE POWER OF RELATIONSHIPS AND THE IMPACT OF A SEED PLANTED
Ramon Chinyoung Sr.

In 1997, I embarked on my football journey as a young child in need of guidance and support from others. Growing up in a single-parent household, my mother and I relocated to Texas when I was just four years old following my parents' divorce. Texas offered us a fresh start, but like many boys raised without a father figure, I often pondered why my life was different from other kids who had their fathers actively involved. At a young age, I began to believe that perhaps I was the problem, and maybe my father simply didn't want anything to do with me.

By the time I turned nine, frustration and anger set in as I struggled to understand why my life was filled with constant challenges—moving from one apartment to another and frequently relocating to find a safe place to call home. I vividly remember those days when my mother and I would walk long distances from grocery stores to our apartment complex, both enduring intense leg pains without complaints. It was during these moments that I realized how much I needed guidance and a male mentor who could provide more than what my hardworking and selfless mother could offer.

That's when football entered my life—a sport that allowed me to express myself, release pent-up frustrations, and be part of a team of young boys led by older role models who, like me, were searching for their place in the world. As a young child, I craved discipline, guidance, and the tools to overcome challenges that seemed insurmountable at the time, not fully understanding how these experiences would shape me in the future.

In 1997, my mother recognized my need for male guidance and enrolled me in a little league football team known as the Northwest Jaguars. Led by men dedicated to making a positive impact on young athletes, this team became instrumental in shaping my character and aspirations during my formative years.

One coach, in particular, Alvin Poole Sr., went above and beyond to support me throughout my early football journey. Coach Poole and his fellow coaches were committed to ensuring that every player attended practice, understanding firsthand the critical role attendance played in our development. I distinctly remember my first year as a Texas high school football head coach in 2018, only to have my dreams sidelined by the sudden onset of Covid-19. With campuses closed and uncertainty looming, securing student athletes' attendance remained paramount for my coaching career's success.

As a young athlete, logistical challenges often interfered with my ability to attend practices due to my mother's work commitments. Fortunately, a coach from the team stepped in, offering daily rides to practice—a seemingly small gesture that made a significant difference in my life. While transportation may seem insignificant to some, for a young man in need of guidance, support, and structure, it was monumental and pivotal in navigating life's obstacles.

Years later, thanks to the unwavering belief and support of my coaches and family, I earned a full athletic scholarship to play collegiate football—an achievement that not only blessed me but also fulfilled my mother's dreams of seeing me graduate from college, especially from an HBCU, play football, and make our family proud. None of this would have been possible without Coach Poole Sr. planting that initial seed of hope and opportunity in me.

Reflecting on my journey, I realized that as a young adult, I had aspirations of playing in the NFL. While my path took a different turn, leading me to volunteer as a coach at my alma mater after college, coaching allowed me to stay connected to the game and give back to the community that supported me. Under the mentorship of Coach Corby Meekins, I began my coaching career in 2012, which provided the stability to support my growing family and lay the foundation for my future.

Transitioning to a head offensive line coach role at Westfield HS in Houston, TX, in 2016 was a defining moment for me. It was an opportunity to pay forward the blessings I received, helping young men overcome their obstacles, achieve academic success, and earn athletic scholarships. Coaches like Justin Outten played a pivotal role in shaping my coaching philosophy—focusing on tough love, discipline, and dedication to empowering young men.

My coaching journey has taught me invaluable lessons about resilience, perseverance, and the profound impact of mentorship. As I ventured into the NFL coaching realm, I realized the importance of passing on the knowledge and guidance I received to the grown men I coach today. Every encounter with a student-athlete holds the potential to impact their lives and, in turn, influence future generations. As I continue to evolve in my coaching career, I remain grateful for the influential figures who shaped my path and the opportunity to inspire others through my experiences.

Whether you're a teacher, coach, campus leader, or principal, you hold a powerful opportunity to positively impact young lives. Even now, as an NFL coach, I draw upon the tools and lessons imparted to me by my mentors to mentor and support the athletes I work with every day.

ABOUT THE AUTHOR:

Social Media:

LinkedIn linkedin.com/in/ramon-chinyoung-sr-70301611a

Email coachchinyoung@gmail.com

Ramon Chinyoung Sr. was born on Feb. 25, 1988, in Houston, Texas. He played as an Offensive Lineman for Southern University from 2007 to 2010. While he did not have professional playing experience, Chinyoung transitioned to coaching, starting as an offensive quality control coach for the Denver Broncos in 2022 before joining the Dallas Cowboys in 2023.

Entering his second season with the Cowboys in 2024, Chinyoung serves as the assistant offensive line coach / quality control. With over 11 years of full-time coaching experience, he brings a wealth of knowledge to the team. Prior to his NFL coaching roles, Chinyoung served as head coach / campus coordinator at Fort Bend Willowridge High School in Houston from 2020 to 2021. During his tenure, he led the Eagles to the Texas High School Football Playoffs in 2020.

Before Willowridge, Chinyoung spent eight successful seasons (2012-2019) at Westfield High School in Houston, Texas. Beginning as an assistant offensive line coach and later becoming assistant head coach, he played a crucial role in the team's impressive record, including a remarkable 58-1 mark in district play and consistent playoff appearances.

Chinyoung earned his bachelor's degree in therapeutic recreation and leisure studies from Southern University, where he was also a standout football player, receiving first-team All-SWAC honors twice and named first-team All-Louisiana in 2009. Outside of football, he enjoys family life with his wife, Morgan Broussard-Chinyoung, and their two sons, Ramon II (RJ) and Myles Henry.

A LITTLE GIRL'S DREAM IN GREENFIELD: FROM CHILDHOOD ASPIRATIONS TO SUPERINTENDENT
Dr. Zandra Jo Galvan

Once a little girl growing up in Greenfield with big dreams, I am now the proud Superintendent of the Greenfield Union School District (GUSD). My journey has been one of profound gratitude, marked by incredible people and transformative partnerships that have ignited my leadership. Since assuming this role in August 2017, my vision has been to create an inclusive and innovative educational environment that prepares every student for future success. This chapter is a tribute to the power of one—a reminder that while one person can spark change, it is through the collective support and collaboration of many that true transformation is achieved. Let this inspire you to believe in your own power to make a difference, to lead with passion, and to uplift those around you with intention and purpose.

My Vision and Mission to Serve

From the outset, my aim was to implement a comprehensive and strategic plan for Greenfield Schools rooted in a sense of urgency to break students free from the cycle of poverty through education. Greenfield is home to 90% of students designated as economically disadvantaged. This visionary plan encompasses our mission, core values, and Board of Trustee priorities, ensuring a unified direction for the district. One vivid memory I hold dear is the day we introduced the practice of visiting a college or university every single year, beginning in preschool, for our students and their families. Witnessing the spark of excitement in their eyes as they realized the potential of planting seeds for their future by attending a university was truly inspiring. This initiative was a collective effort driven by our shared commitment to excellence and ignited a fire within our team to take impactful steps toward achieving remarkable results.

Innovation Through Partnerships

One of the most thrilling aspects of my role has been forging transformative partnerships that bring innovative opportunities to our students. Collaborations with organizations like Digital Promise's League of Innovative Schools, Verizon Innovative Learning partnerships, Apple Education, Google Education, eSports Laboratories, FIRST Robotics Leagues, and LEGO Education have revolutionized learning in Greenfield. I distinctly remember the excitement of taking students to visit Apple's campus, where they met CEO Tim Cook. Their palpable enthusiasm and curiosity as they explored cutting-edge technologies and discussed their dreams with industry leaders broadened their horizons and inspired them to envision careers in technology and beyond. Let this motivate you to set bold goals, embrace strategic planning with partners, and relentlessly pursue excellence for students.

We have successfully created opportunities for students to tour the world, led to the launch of eSports labs, virtual reality experiences, Drone clubs for "Girls to Fly" and "Boys to Soar," and eSports competitions, which have become key vehicles for project-based learning and problem-solving skills. These partnerships not only enhance learning but also inspire students to dream big and pursue their aspirations. Let this encourage you to seek out and cultivate innovative partnerships that can open new doors and expand horizons for those you lead.

Commitment to Equity and Inclusivity

My unwavering commitment to ensuring that every student is prepared socially, emotionally, and academically for college and career success is the cornerstone of my leadership. The mantra "ALL Means ALL" reflects our dedication to inclusivity and equity. Establishing Social-Emotional Learning (SEL) and wellness spaces across our schools was a deeply personal mission for me. Growing up in Greenfield, I experienced firsthand the challenges of a farm-working community. I knew that creating supportive environments was crucial for our students' success. These efforts, driven by the dedication of our educators, staff, and community members, have inspired a culture where every student is valued and supported.

We have added SEL and wellness spaces, shifted to 21st-century classroom furniture in all spaces, and focused on student-centered LEGO and Apple learning and maker spaces at all schools to build, innovate, and prepare for successful postsecondary college and career futures. These initiatives ensure that all students have the resources and support they need to thrive. Let this inspire you to champion equity and inclusivity in all your endeavors, ensuring that everyone has the opportunity to succeed.

Cultivating a Positive School Culture

Creating a positive and collaborative school culture has been one of my proudest achievements. Our harmonious working environment, where grievances and contract violations with labor union partners are virtually non-existent, is a testament to the collaborative spirit of our district. One personal story that stands out is when a teacher approached me to share how much she appreciated the transparent and open communication we fostered. She felt truly valued and supported, which motivated her to give her best every day. This positive culture is the result of mutual respect among all stakeholders, including teachers, administrators, classified staff, and the community. Together, we have built a supportive and productive educational environment that continues to inspire and innovate.

"When the superintendent sets the tone, the directors, the C-suite, the board, the principals, the teachers, our classified labor partners all share that. We have really great culture here in Greenfield that we've cultivated over the last seven years." Let this motivate you to foster a positive and collaborative culture wherever you lead, understanding that it starts with setting the right tone and building mutual respect so that our teams choose to stay.

Inspiring Young Children and Youth

One of the most fulfilling aspects of my role has been inspiring young children and youth to become future leaders. I vividly recall my own days as a young student in Greenfield schools, harboring big dreams despite the challenges around me. By providing students with opportunities to engage in innovative programs and exposing them to various career paths, we empower them to dream big and achieve their goals. Watching our students grow, succeed, and lead has been one of the greatest rewards of my career, including witnessing many of my former students returning to Greenfield as teachers and school principals under my leadership. Their success stories remind me of my own journey and the importance of nurturing their greatest potential.

At an elementary career day, I met a little girl named Ruby. She approached me with wide eyes and an infectious smile, saying, "I want to be a superintendent just like you!" Ruby's determination and enthusiasm reminded me of my younger self. It brings me immense joy to see little girls who look like me, who share my heritage, being inspired to dream big and believe in their own immense potential. Let this inspire you to invest in the next generation, nurturing their dreams and providing them with the tools they need to lead and succeed.

The Power of Relationships to Transform Lives

The power of relationships in transforming lives cannot be overstated. Building strong, supportive relationships with students, staff, and the community has been central to our success at GUSD. A memorable interaction was with a student who had been struggling academically and emotionally. Through consistent support and encouragement, he began to thrive. This experience reinforced my belief in the transformative power of relationships. By fostering a sense of belonging and connection, we have created a district where collaboration and mutual support are the norm. These relationships are the foundation of our thriving, positive school culture and the key to unlocking the full potential of every individual in our community. Let this inspire you to prioritize building and nurturing strong relationships in all aspects of your life and leadership, understanding their profound impact on personal and collective success.

Embracing a Positive Mindset

A positive mindset has been crucial in leading my life and career. It has empowered me to face challenges with resilience and view obstacles as opportunities for growth. One particularly challenging period was during my pursuit of a doctoral degree while managing my responsibilities as superintendent and balancing time with my family and children. Maintaining a positive outlook helped me navigate this demanding journey successfully. I encourage you to adopt a positive mindset, as it can transform your approach to challenges and inspire those around you to do the same.

Personal Journey and Family Tribute

Balancing my role as superintendent with my pursuit of a doctoral degree at the University of Southern California has been one of my greatest rewards. My dedication to education is matched by my commitment to my family, who have been my unwavering support system. My parents, Helen and Joe N. Zamora, instilled in me the values of hard work and perseverance. My mom, in particular, always encouraged me to live boldly and never dim my light for anyone. Although she passed away recently, she continues to be my inspiration. My 92-year-old father is still my inspiration today and fully participated in my doctoral ceremony. My husband, Javier, and our children, Zoe, Zia, and Zachary, continue to inspire and motivate me every day. My family's love and support have been the foundation of my career. Additionally, my big sisters and brothers have always supported and loved their little sister, cheering me on every step of my life.

As a proud Latina, I recognize the importance of representation and the power of my heritage. Earning my doctorate and going far in education is attributed to showing other Latinos/Latinas that it can be done. Organizations like the California Association of Latino/a/x Superintendents and Administrators (CALSA) and the Association of Latino Administrators and Superintendents (ALAS) have been instrumental in shaping my leadership journey. Their support, along with the guidance and inspiration from Digital Promise, national superintendent organizations like AASA, and District Administration, has empowered me and many others to lead with purpose and passion. Let this inspire you to honor your heritage, value the support of your loved ones, and seek out organizations that can help you grow and lead with impact.

Overcoming Gatekeepers

Throughout my journey, I encountered gatekeepers who doubted my capabilities and tried to hinder my progress. Their resistance only fueled my determination to succeed. By overcoming these obstacles, I demonstrated that perseverance and resilience are key to achieving one's goals. My experience has taught me the importance of believing in oneself and staying true to one's vision, even in the face of adversity. Let this motivate you to remain steadfast in your pursuits, knowing that resilience and determination can overcome any barrier.

The Power of Storytelling

Storytelling has been a powerful tool in my journey, allowing me to connect with others and inspire change. Sharing personal stories helps others see the possibilities within themselves and ignites the spark of hope and determination. My story, from a little girl in Greenfield to Superintendent, has resonated with many, including young Ruby, who now dreams of following in my footsteps. Let this inspire you to share your story, as it has the power to touch lives, build connections, and inspire others to pursue their dreams.

The Power of Social Media

Social media has been a powerful tool in branding our district and connecting with a broader audience. Through platforms like Twitter and LinkedIn, I have been able to share our district's achievements and initiatives, meet influential leaders like Tim Cook, and highlight the positive impact of our programs. This visibility has not only enhanced our district's reputation but also inspired others to adopt similar innovative practices. Connecting with organizations like Apple was a game-changer for the children of Greenfield, who got out of our small farm-working community to meet with several San Francisco parts at an evening of inspiration. My message to everyone there that night was, that everybody has a story, when you discover your story then you discover your purpose in life. I asked everyone to ask my brilliant scholars about their story and to tell them your story. Let this inspire you to leverage social media to share your story, connect with others, and amplify your impact.

Be the Power of One

Reflecting on my journey from a little girl in Greenfield to the Superintendent of the Greenfield Union School District, I am reminded of the immense power each of us holds to make a difference, one child at a time. My story is a testament to the impact of individual efforts and the boundless potential within each of us. This is a call to action: use your own life's journey to live fully in each moment and be the power of one.

Every step you take, no matter how small, has the potential to ignite change. Embrace your unique story, for it is a source of strength and inspiration. Believe in your potential, for it is limitless. Recognize that within you lies the power to inspire those around you, to uplift and to transform lives.

Remember, the path to greatness is paved with small acts of kindness, moments of courage, and unwavering determination. Be the mentor, the guide, the friend who believes in others when they struggle to believe in themselves. Stand up for what is right, even when it is not easy. Your actions, your words, and your presence can create ripples that extend far beyond what you can see.

You have the power to change the world. Live your life with purpose, passion, and perseverance. Inspire those around you by being the best version of yourself. Together, we can build a future where every child believes in their worth, every individual realizes their potential, and every community thrives.

Be the power of one. Embrace your journey, and let your story be a beacon of hope and inspiration. Together, we can create a legacy of positive change that will echo through generations.

ABOUT THE AUTHOR:

Social Media:

LinkedIn linkedin.com/zandrajogalvan
Facebook facebook.com/zandrajogalvan
Email zjgalvan@yahoo.com

Dr. Zandra Jo Galvan has served as Superintendent of the Greenfield Union School District since August 10, 2017, bringing with her over 28 years of experience in public education. Her journey began as an elementary classroom teacher within GUSD, where she had attended school from kindergarten through graduation—an opportunity that allowed her childhood dreams to come full circle. In her tenure, spanning seven years, Dr. Galvan has spearheaded the implementation of the GUSD District Strategic Plan, aligning it with an LCAP-driven vision, mission, core values, and Board of Trustee priorities. Under her leadership, she has introduced a PLC model emphasizing essential standards, learning targets, common formative assessments, and rigorous data analysis.

Recognizing the importance of career technical education and job market trends, Dr. Galvan has mapped out industry sectors to better prepare students for successful postsecondary college and career paths. She has also championed the integration of Social-Emotional Learning (SEL) and wellness spaces across all schools, alongside the transition to 21st-century classroom furniture. Driven by a commitment to innovation, she has established student-centered Esports, LEGO, and Apple learning spaces district-wide, fostering an environment conducive to creativity and future readiness.

Dr. Galvan leads GUSD as a nationally recognized Digital Promise/League of Innovative Schools District, prioritizing equity and inclusivity for all students. Her dedication to educational leadership has been further acknowledged through prestigious honors such as the inaugural Global Silicon Valley Google National Fellowship in 2023-24, alongside 24 other esteemed national fellows.

Superintendent Galvan earned her B.A. in Liberal Studies and Teaching Credential from Fresno State, followed by an M.A. in Curriculum and Instruction from CSU Monterey Bay. She later attained an M.A. and Administrative Credential in Educational Leadership from San Jose State University, culminating in her recent Doctorate from USC in May 2024. Complementing her academic achievements, Dr. Galvan has successfully completed the Association of California School Administrators (ACSA) Superintendent Academy and actively contributes as a member of several prominent educational councils and boards, including ACSA Superintendents Council, CSBA Superintendents' Council, and the National Superintendents Roundtable.

Dr. Galvan's leadership extends nationally as a mentor, advisor, and presenter for aspiring female and Latino/a/x superintendents through organizations like AASA, Future Ready, and ALL4ED Schools. She serves on the National District Administration Superintendent Advisory team and holds positions on the ACSA Region 10 Board of Directors and the ALAS Board of Directors for 2023-2025, having previously served as CALSA Immediate Past President (2021-2023) for California.

Throughout her career, Dr. Galvan has been honored with several accolades, including the RTM Innovative Superintendent Technology Award in 2022, CALSA State Superintendent of the Year for Region 4 in 2022, ACSA Dr. William Barr Superintendent of the Year for Region 10 in both 2020 and 2022, the ACSA Region 10 Blanche Montague Inspiring Woman Superintendent of the Year in 2023, the Keith Parkhurst Leadership Award in 2024, and most recently, the ALAS National Superintendent of the Year for 2023-2024.

Passionate about ensuring every student is socially, emotionally, and academically prepared for college and career success, Dr. Galvan fosters a culture within GUSD where every team member is recognized as an elite contributor dedicated to breaking the cycle of poverty through education. Her unwavering commitment to "ALL Means ALL" embodies the Greenfield

Guarantee, ensuring that every student in the Greenfield Union School District receives equitable opportunities to thrive.

ABOUT THE LEAD AUTHOR

Chip Baker is a fourth-generation educator. He has been a teacher/coach for over twenty-five years. He is a multiple time best-selling Author, Youtuber/Podcaster, Transformational Speaker and Life Coach.

Chip Baker is the creator of the Youtube channel/podcast "Chip Baker - The Success Chronicles" where he interviews people of all walks of life and shares their stories for positive inspiration and motivation.

Live. Learn. Serve. Inspire. Go get it!

Email: chipbakertsc@gmail.com
Wrote By Me: https://www.wroteby.me/chipbaker
Online Store:
http://chip-baker-the-success-chronicles.square.site/
Facebook Page:
https://www.facebook.com/TSCChipBaker
Instagram: @chipbakertsc
LinkedIn:
https://www.linkedin.com/in/chipbakerthesuccesschronicles/
Twitter: @chipbaker19

Chip Baker—The Success Chronicles
YouTube: youtube.com/c/ChipBakerTheSuccessChronicles
Podcast: https://anchor.fm/chip-baker

Other Books:
Growing Through Your Go Through
Effective Conversation To Ignite Relationships
Suited For Success Vol. 2
The Formula Chart For Life
The Impact of influence
The Impact of Influence Vol. 2
Kids Book- Stay On The Right P.A.T.H.
The Impact of Influence Vol. 3
Black Men Love
The Impact of Influence Vol. 4
The Winning Mindset
The Impact of Influence Vol. 5
Concrete Connections
The Impact of Influence Vol. 6
Voices For Leadership: Embracing Diverse Strategies for Effective Leadership
Sole Searching: Daily Devotional for Sneakerheads
It's Not About Me
The Impact of Influence Vol. 7

Online Store

PICK UP THESE OTHER TITLES BY CHIP BAKER

GROWING THROUGH YOUR GO THROUGH

EFFECTIVE CONVERSATION TO IGNITE RELATIONSHIP

SUITED FOR SUCCESS: VOLUME 2

THE FORMULA CHART FOR LIFE

THE IMPACT OF INFLUENCE: VOLUME 1

THE IMPACT OF INFLUENCE: VOLUME 2

R.O.C.K. SOLID

STAY ON THE RIGHT P.A.T.H.

THE IMPACT OF INFLUENCE: VOLUME 3

BLACK MEN LOVE

THE IMPACT OF INFLUENCE: VOLUME 4

THE WINNING MINDSET

THE IMPACT OF INFLUENCE: VOLUME 5

CONCRETE CONNECTIONS

THE IMPACT OF INFLUENCE: VOLUME 6

IT'S NOT ABOUT ME

SOLE SEARCHING

VOICES FOR LEADERSHIP

To order your autographed copies visit
http://chip-baker-the-success-chronicles.square.site,

Made in the USA
Columbia, SC
24 July 2024

38636516R00061